Wings of Power

BOEING AND THE POLITICS
OF GROWTH IN THE NORTHWEST

Wings of Power

BOEING AND THE POLITICS
OF GROWTH IN THE NORTHWEST

T. M. SELL

University of Washington Press

Seattle and London

Library of Congress Cataloging-in-Publication Data

Sell, T. M.

    Wings of power : Boeing and the politics of growth in the Northwest / T.M. Sell.

    p. cm.

    Includes bibliographical references and index.

    ISBN 0-295-98049-4

    1. Boeing Company—History. 2. Aircraft industry—United States—History. 3. Aircraft industry—United States—Employees. 4. Aeronautics, Commercial—United States—History. 5. Seattle Metropolitan Area (Wash.)—Economic conditions. I. Title.

    HD9711.U63 B6364 2001

    338.7′629133′0973—dc21   00-060702

For my parents, who taught me to learn,
and for Nancy, who has since supported that habit

Contents

Preface ix

Acknowledgments xiii

Prologue: Power, Politics, and Growth xv

1 / The Runway: Boeing Drops a Bomb 3

2 / Come Fly with Us: A Short History of Boeing and Seattle 12

3 / Flight Path: Growth and Antigrowth 33

4 / Full Court Press: Boeing Confronts the Paradox 52

5 / Paper Airplanes in the Marble Zoo: Boeing and the Legislature 60

6 / Things Happen: A Tale of Several Cities 74

Renton 78

Everett 85

7 / Calling in the Cavalry 95

8 / Soft Landing 102

Epilogue: Growth and Antigrowth, Revisited 114

Notes 125

Bibliography 148

Index 160

Preface

I FIRST BECAME AWARE of Boeing when I realized that that was where my father went every night, around 11:00 P.M. He went to school during the day, and then, like a lot of people, he went to Boeing. That he actually made money by going to work was a little beyond me; I was about five years old. Several people on the block worked at Boeing, or had; my mother eventually ended up there too. Everywhere you went, you ran into somebody who did work or had worked at Boeing.

I next took notice of Boeing at about the time of the locally famous Boeing Bust of 1969-71. My father had moved on to teaching college by then, but my stepfather's employer, Heath Tecna, was (and is, through several changes of ownership) a significant Boeing supplier. Like the founder of Heath, my stepfather was an ex-Boeing employee. The Heath stock my stepfather had so assiduously bought plummeted to less than a dollar; the air of giddy anticipation that had pervaded our household turned to something more somber.

When I was fourteen I started to come to grips with what Boeing meant to the Puget Sound region. For social studies class I performed a survey of gasoline prices at local stations, having long heard that station owners raised their prices every two weeks when Boeing workers got paid. Over several weeks, I carefully noted the daily prices at a half dozen stations on the bus route to and from school and learned that the legend was indeed true: as surely as the tides, the gas prices rose a few cents every two weeks right on Boeing's payday, then fell by the beginning of the next week. One service station manager even admitted as much, though most were not too keen on talking to a beginning social scientist.[1]

In my life and the lives of the people from my area, Boeing was The Thing That Always Was. Boeing was the reason you ended vacations early; it was the thing that made your neighbors stop spending money and study listlessly for new careers while waiting to get called back. Boys from the 'hood a little older than I recall shuffling out of class at Renton High School, in the name of safety, when the 707s first flew overhead. An out-of-state editor of mine once expressed surprise and concern that this airport, Renton Field, emptied out over the high school. But people around here would probably get more concerned if aircraft were not overhead.

Eventually other members of my family, and many friends, went to work for Boeing. When I wrote about Boeing for local newspapers I couldn't walk through a plant without running into somebody I knew from school or the gym or somewhere. For decades, Seattle styled itself the Jet City, and Boeing and its fortunes were the waves we all seemed to ride.

Seattle was a big city before Boeing came along, but Boeing put it on the world map as well as the Washington State one. When I lived overseas in the 1970s, foreigners had heard of Boeing but not Seattle; when I traveled to Europe again for the big air shows in Paris and London in the mid-1990s, saying I was from Seattle opened doors and secured interviews. (I especially recall the reaction of some Russian aerospace officials with limited English [though far better than my Russian]: "Ah, Seattle!" they said. "I was inmate in Seattle," confided one. I'm still not sure what he meant.)

But in the late 1980s someone at a party said something I had never heard before. "I don't understand why there's so much Boeing news in the paper," said the person, a transplant. "What's the big deal?" Something had changed, and at that moment something was changing. A relationship riveted in high-test aluminum was working loose in a way the casual observer might not expect. Boeing, the apparent raison d'être of the Puget Sound country, was about to have a falling out with its hosts.

At first glance, it might seem like a remarkable thing that the world's largest company town was treating its prime employer poorly. Certainly no existing political theory on the left or the right would predict that such a thing would happen, and political practice usually dictates against making things hard for big employers. But structural forces in the local political economy made this almost inevitable, forces that I call the Paradox of Growth.

The Seattle area had grown a lot in the fifty years that Boeing had been part of the landscape, both by design and by accident. Indeed, the region, like most others in the United States, had spent a lot of time, money, and energy trying to grow, trying to diversify and expand its economy as well as trying to help Boeing succeed.

The forces behind this have been aptly called "the growth machine" or "the growth coalition" by a number of observers. It is a longstanding fixture of local politics across the country. Particularly people in real estate, retail, the media, and housing development all benefit from a growing local population. And the community at large can benefit, because a larger population will spur more offerings in everything from arts to shopping. Too much growth, on the other hand, can degrade the quality of life, producing bad air and water, loss of open space, higher housing prices, congested roads, and overcrowded schools. This eventually produces an antigrowth coalition, usually calling for "slow growth" or "sensible growth," attractive but amorphous terms.

But this is where my story diverges from that of most other observers, many of whom go no further than criticizing unbridled drives for growth. The antigrowth coalition, typically a coalition of middle- and upper-class interests whose livelihoods do not appear to depend on more growth, can succeed at changing the game to make growth more difficult. In our example, Washington State—prodded by antigrowth forces—jumped into the fray, legislating a Growth Management Act to try to control growth. This came at a time when communities around the country were mortgaging their souls to get factories to locate nearby.

This act, and similar initiatives and philosophies at the local level, raised Boeing's local costs enough that it threatened, if not to relocate, to grow elsewhere in the future. Moreover, if the region developed a reputation as a difficult, expensive place to do business, other firms would leave, and new firms would choose to locate elsewhere. That is the paradox: cities and regions work like ants to make their areas grow. Eventually, the growth becomes so great that growth and the responses it engenders combine to drive new growth away and cause contraction.

Existing theories of political power and growth politics do not account for this, but the hundreds of growth-management initiatives to be found in cities, states, and counties all across the country are evidence that it is true. It is a conundrum that puts citizens, governments, and business interests at odds in ways that were rarely seen until the last few decades. Government officials must balance constituents' need for jobs against their need for quality of life, even as citizens and businesses face that same question. It is a problem without easy answers, one that challenges communities to engage in a kind of visionary political management that is too rarely seen in millennial America.

This is the story of how this happened in Washington State, and what it meant to Boeing and to the Greater Seattle area. In Seattle, the experience of Boeing and of the various layers of state and local government challenges many widely held assumptions about Boeing's role in the region and about the power of business elites in metropolitan communities. It is a story about wealth and power and jobs, a story that is still playing itself out. It is a story about politics, and about people.

Acknowledgments

THIS PROJECT could not have been completed without the assistance of a number of people. Professor Donald J. McCrone first suggested the topic, at a time when I was unsure where to go. He and the other members of my dissertation committee at the University of Washington, Professors David J. Olson and Donald R. Matthews, provided considerable advice and encouragement along the way. Professor Christine DiStefano helped me understand the importance and application of theory through several courses in my years at the University. Thanks also to my colleagues at Highline College, especially Professors Phil Droke and Robin Buchan, who let me try out portions of this as guest lecturer in their classes. And thanks especially to the editors at the University of Washington Press, especially Michael P. Duckworth, who made this a book and not a list of what I did in graduate school, and Richard von Kleinsmid for his thorough and careful editing of the manuscript.

People who have made a difference do not get thanked enough, I think. Let me make note, then, of some who got me interested in politics and social science, and helped me along the path toward thinking all the way through things, instead of just reacting to them: Professors Ken Dolbeare, Greg Weeks, Charles Nisbet, and Russ Lidman of The Evergreen State College; professors Eugene Hogan and Lyle Harris of Western Washington University; and Professors Kerslake and Keyes of Renton High School.

Sincere thanks go to my editors and colleagues at *Valley Daily News*, including Jack Mayne, who made me a business writer when I was again at a loss for what to do next, and Robert Jones, who let me write all the Boeing stories I could stand; and to many people I worked with in my all-too-brief stint at the *Seattle Post-Intelligencer,* especially John Levesque and Don Smith, who were invaluable in letting me pursue research on this project while working there. My friends at the *Everett Herald,* Kathie Anderson and Dale Folkerts, provided enormous help in pointing me toward sources both in and outside the paper.

Many people in local and state government also cooperated by discussing their dealings with Boeing at length, as did many people within Boeing. Special thanks go to Sherry Nebel and Russ Young at Boeing, without whose continual lobbying and assistance most of the Boeing interviews would have been impossible. And thanks, of course, to my parents and my wife, Nancy, without whose encouragement and support this project might never have taken true flight.

To these many people, and more, go much of the credit for what works on these pages. The mistakes are mine.

Prologue

Power, Politics, and Growth

Among the concerns of political science, none has been witness to more tortured debates than power. Bloodied critiques litter the field; the combat has been bitter.

—Sidney Plotkin, 1991

In all political systems of the world, much of politics is economics, and most of economics is also politics.

—Charles Lindblom, 1977

THIS BOOK is about community power—who is powerful in any metropolitan region, why, and what it means for all of us. It is also about what is becoming the preeminent issue for communities and the source of many community power struggles: growth. It might be helpful to set some terms, and understand what has been said before about this subject.

Before you talk about power, you have to say what it is you are talking about. And it is not enough to say, as a U.S. Supreme Court justice once said of pornography, "I know it when I see it." Power matters in the present exploration because a big company such as Boeing is widely assumed to be politically powerful, and counted as dominant in its own back yard. If that is true, it raises serious questions about how growth management could happen under Boeing's nose.

What is power? Does tangible influence equal power? Does mere persuasion qualify? How can power be measured? How much power does a large, private entity such as Boeing possess at any given moment? And how does it gain or lose power relative to other political players such as legislators, interest groups, competing organizations, and the public at large? How can we say with any certainty when any one group or faction or company has "too much power"? The answers are neither easy nor simple.

In certain respects, power is a phantom. For all its labels it cannot be bottled or packaged, and it weighs no more than a political actor's last triumph. Put simply, power is the ability to get things done through brute force or gentle persuasion, to have one's voice heard, to make a difference, even marginal, in the making of public and private decisions.

It seems there must be some threat of punishment, some promise of reward for power to have any tangible reality. Coercion underlies many social interactions, such as speed limits or taxes. But not everyone who obeys the speed limit must be coerced, just as some people volunteer to help the poor even though they pay taxes, in part, to support them. Does a large company, such as Boeing, rely on the power to coerce? One cannot wander the halls of Boeing without a badge, and its security force is armed. But that is not what earns it tax breaks from local government. Is it instead persuasion, as evidenced by campaign contributions and lobbying? It is true that by threatening to relocate production elsewhere, Boeing is using some coercion, but it also uses promise and persuasion by reminding policy makers of the economic benefits if it chooses to stay. If a group is successful at achieving some of its goals, or even in partially altering the outcomes of other competitions, can it not be said to be powerful, especially if its counsel is always heard?

Social scientists have kicked around a lot of specific notions of power, from direct power to influence to agenda control to the ability to keep somebody else from making a decision.[1] But however much power might depend on relationships and perspectives, parts of it—such as money and jobs—are quite tangible.

Power is unevenly distributed across the political landscape. Various individuals and groups—interests—are in competition over power and the spoils it represents. The power of groups in opposition to each other and to the government is an essential element of democracy, one cited by both James Madison and Alexis de Tocqueville long ago. From the first non-native settlers, through the founding fathers, on down, Americans have tended to be more than a little mistrustful of the notion of individuals and small groups having and wielding power. Federalism, the essence of our form of republican government, was specifically designed with the idea of so fracturing the government that it would be difficult for any one faction to dominate political decision making. State and local government are part of that division of power, important stones in the edifice of American government. Those governments are fractured even further, between judicial, legislative, and executive functions. Nonetheless, critics, researchers, and analysts throughout the nation's history have asked whether factions (often referred to as interest groups, or special interest groups by those who do not like them) are not capable of subverting at least part of the government to their specific ends.

Three basic models of analysis may help us understand and analyze power relations between groups: Marxist, pluralist, and elitist. Although out of vogue in many places (including nearly all the nations that have ever adopted Marxist practice), Marxist analysis retains a certain cachet for those on the American left. The classic Marxist view is that power is based on class interests, with capitalists largely on one side and workers on the other.[2] The state is mere superstructure, existing only to further the aims of the wealthy class. The Marxist assumption is that commercial interests exercise hegemony over society (because, in classic Marxist terms, they control the means of production), and that government's chief function is to legitimize and extend capitalist control. In the Marxist explanation, Boeing accrues capital by milking its handmaiden, government, and its workers for all they are worth.

The Marxist model has, at a minimum, an intuitive logic: government (in the United States if not elsewhere) spends a lot of time and money ensuring that the market economy continues to function. Private interests recognize this and try to rig the rules for their own ends. The state therefore becomes the fulcrum for an ongoing competition between a host of players (businesses, consumers, workers, and government itself), each seeking the greatest reward from the system. Contrary to what most Marxists say, market competition does exist and is important, but competition outside the market is equally wide-ranging and intense.

According to Marxist theory, the capitalist economy's inability to provide adequate jobs, goods, and housing for the masses is part flaw and part tactic; the capitalist class creates a permanent underclass so as to keep workers pliable and thereby provide a ready supply of cheap labor. That such an underclass would be largely unable to buy the products that the capitalist class produces is a real concern, but it also suggests that capitalists would have to be especially myopic. Sometimes, no doubt, they are, but there is precious little evidence that capitalists are either a cohesive class or engaged in a policy of economic subjugation. You don't need class theory to explain why employers seek to keep wage costs down any more than you need capitalist theory to explain why workers want the highest possible wages. Everybody wants more.

Marxists will quibble about this point and that one, endlessly, like Energizer bunnies in red. But strict adherence to the cant of the current canon is unimportant. The Marxist analysis is ultimately unsatisfactory. Too many instances arise where the capitalist monolith finds itself rent by internal competition, where the state acts in ways that can only be described as detrimental to capitalist interests, and where workers, consumers, and voters exhibit power of their own. In particular, in Boeing's case, state and local government kept acting in somebody else's interest, a result not predicted by the Marxist model.

Elitism is, in some ways, the intellectual stepchild of Marxism, arguing that power is held by a relatively small group of interests who have wealth and status, and whose influence over social and government institutions lets them make rules and control agendas. We find here a concern (similar to Marxism's) with the power of large, privately controlled enterprise, but the elitist solutions would involve more (but not total) government control over the economy, and not necessarily less democracy. In the elitist model, Boeing is among the small group of moneyed interests that dominate the state and public discourse. As we shall see below, in a lot of what has been written about Boeing, Seattle, and Washington, that is the common assumption.

At the municipal level, a lot of attention has been focused on the "growth coalition" of realtors, bankers, media moguls, and land developers, active in most cities in the United States, who seek only after economic expansion for the obvious monetary benefits it will bring them.[3] In the growth coalition, elite theorists have identified a key player, but not the only player, as the pluralists often note.

Elite theory's preoccupation with the growth machine may blind it to the often competitive nature of the system. While it is correct that not all growth is good and that growth is not a panacea, some, such as John R. Logan and Harvey L. Moloch, ascribe too much power to the growth coalition:

> The pursuit of exchange values so permeates the life of localities that cities become organized as enterprises devoted to the increase of aggregate rent levels through the intensification of land use. The city becomes, in effect, a "growth machine." The growth ethic pervades virtually all aspects of local

life, including the political system, the agenda for economic development and even cultural organizations like baseball teams and museums.[4]

G. William Domhoff argues that the growth machine "is the most over-represented group on city councils, as numerous studies show...."[5] For a long time, that was true. The most recent of those studies is from 1970; the rest are from 1964 and earlier. Things do change. Domhoff acknowledges that the growth machine does not always win, and he does distinguish between "the power elite" (industrial capitalists) and the growth machine (development interests). But, like Logan and Molotch, he fails to recognize the possibility that the two sides could be in conflict.[6] Even a noted elite theorist such as Thomas R. Dye recognizes the potential for conflict among elite factions:

But consensus on behalf of economic growth is sometimes challenged by entrenched community interests. However much the "growth machine" elite may strive for consensus, and despite the admonitions of scholars that economic growth benefits the whole community, some people do not like growth. Indeed, it has become fashionable in upper middle-class circles today to complain loudly about the problems created by growth—congestion, pollution, noise, unsightly development, the replacement of green spaces with concrete slabs. People who already own their houses and do not intend to sell them, people whose jobs are secure in bureaucracies or tenured professorships, people who may be displaced from their homes and neighborhoods by new facilities, people who see no direct benefit to themselves from growth, and businesses or industries who fear new competition which growth may bring to the community all combine to form a potentially powerful counter-elite.[7]

San Francisco is a perfect example. A diverse group of activists there united to derail the city's growth machine. "The progrowth coalition of downtown business elites, labor unions and city hall officials that controlled the city's economic and physical development for a quarter of a century is now in pieces, its vision for San Francisco discarded, its relentless building of high rises checked, its hegemony in land use and development erased."[8] Why? Richard Edward DeLeon tends to celebrate the defeat of the growth machine as a triumph of good over evil, and he only gets close to what really drove the outcome:

The progrowth regime accomplished much, for better and for worse. It changed the face of San Francisco. In doing so, however, it fostered resistance among those the regime threatened or whose own dreams for the city were ignored. In dialectical fashion, the progrowth regime created the conditions that gave rise to its nemesis, the slow growth movement.[9]

The color of DeLeon's exploration paints the whole scenario as a triumph of the downtrodden over the antichrist. In some sense, perhaps it is. But it is more a case of one group getting theirs ahead of another group. To paint one victory or another with the hue of virtue does no service to the goal of seeking an outcome that gives everybody something worth having. Only occasionally does DeLeon note that the growth machine, which fostered a service economy, created a "post-materialist" middle class for whom more growth was, at best, an ambivalent prospect.[10]

This is, in essence, the pluralist model: different groups compete at different times over different issues—no single interest runs the show. Elite theorists frequently denigrate pluralism, though they tend to misunderstand it. Robert Dahl, the researcher most associated with the pluralist approach, says pluralism in no way precludes—nor was meant to preclude—the idea that power will be distributed unevenly. On the contrary, he says inequality is an endemic condition of any polyarchal (democratic) system.[11] Pluralism is to political science as Keynesianism is to economics: rarely understood and usually improperly applied.[12] In the pluralist model, Boeing is simply one entity competing with many others for the spoils of modern life. It is a big, powerful player, but not the only one.

One of the important actors in the public drama is the state, a point missed by many Marxist and elite analysts. Because of the state's particular need (the state in this context means any relevant level of government), it may appear that it is little more than the scut-boy of private enterprise. But it is not that simple. Whereas business people are driven by profit, local officials are motivated by electoral concerns.[13] Why? Rather than being the spawn of the growth machine, modern city councils and mayoral offices tend to be dominated by people without careers apart from government. To be unelected, for many elected officials, is to be unemployed. City politicians' careers are dependent on the economy because if it suffers, they will get booted. And they know this.

In the mind of the politician or development official the benefits that flow from such [private capital] investment are quite clear. Investment generates jobs. Jobs mean fewer unemployed people, lower cost government, and a more robust employment multiplier.[14]

That so many social scientists seem to have trouble grasping this idea is curious; to anyone who has actually watched local politics, it is a "gee-whiz" notion. Even when incumbents survive elections that occur amid recessions, at a minimum they will have to pursue altered policy choices in their next terms. The economy is not always the issue; sometimes things are going well, in which case the issue often is growth management. But it is always the issue just below the surface.

A growing economy also is important to cities because they frequently raise money via bond sales to the private sector; investors tend to buy bonds from cities that are "growing economically" and to avoid those in decline.

The result is that, for a city to market its bonds at reasonable interest rates, it must be attentive to what the bond "community" thinks of its economic prospects. This, in turn, means that city officials must be deeply attentive to demonstrating that they are fiscally conservative and interested in stimulating local growth and in presiding over a city that will continue to be economically vibrant. A reputation for being anti-business, for not listening to local businessmen's schemes for making a greater city, is an invitation to fiscal trouble that even the hardiest progressive politicians are unlikely to accept.[15]

While disparaging municipal drives for growth, most elite theorists also overlook the importance of jobs. Or, as one economic development talking head put it, "It's a lot easier to manage growth than it is to manage contraction." Have no doubt: the benefits of growth are regularly overstated by its proponents; the jobs are never as plentiful, the tax collections and spin-off opportunities never as golden. But when jobs leave, the price can be heavy, in human as well as fiscal terms. And every job means somebody the city does not have to support, or find a job for. This is what Seattle-area officials have in mind when they are paying attention to Boeing's wishes, because the essential jobs are primary jobs, export jobs, jobs not tied to local consumption:

Export industries create jobs and wealth at the expense of consumers residing in other regions. Hence they transfer wealth to the city from elsewhere.

The potential loss of such major manufacturing capacity would be a severe blow to the wealth-creating capacity of the industrial city, whereas the acquisition of one can yield substantial "spillover" benefits to the local economy in the form of employment, construction and retail sales.[16]

For such industries, the aims of the growth coalition are at best tangential, and the externalities of growth may be detrimental to firms with national and world markets. Export firms (and this just means exporting out of the area, not necessarily out of the country) do not benefit from higher land values (and may in fact be hurt by them if the firms wish to expand locally). Nor do they benefit from traffic congestion, nor are their workers necessarily advantaged by higher home prices. Members of the growth coalition, such as retailers, newspapers, and developers, certainly benefit from high wages often paid by manufacturers, but it is largely a one-way relationship. The two sides may even find occasional common ground on topics such as regulation, but even this is marginal, for the kinds of regulation that help one group may in fact hurt the other. As Bryan D. Jones and Lynn W. Bachelor point out in their study of General Motors and Detroit, the initial organizers of opposition to GM's proposed Poletown plant were business people who hoped to redevelop the area themselves.[17]

So city officials are regularly faced with conflicting demands: a growth coalition that wants an open road; an industrial sector that wants minimal interference in its affairs and sufficient quality of life for its workers (industrial and especially high-tech executives regularly mention quality of life as a key issue, because it is an essential tool for recruiting and retaining skilled workers); and a mass electorate that will want more or less and a little of everything. And the whims of unelected municipal bureaucrats frequently are a wild card in policy discussion and implementation.[18]

The importance of jobs often puts industrialists in a dominant position relative to city officials. As many analysts have noted, capital is mobile and cities are not. The cost of acquiring information often leaves cities at a disadvantage in trying to figure just what it will take to get a factory to move in or stay.[19] But big cities, and states, with more resources, tend to be at less of a disadvantage than smaller cities. And skillful political leaders are not without chips to play of their own.

The state can be seen as a forum within which competing or conflicting social forces contend, as well as an institution with the powers to compel obedience. Environmentalists, farmers, workers and many other groups contend with business for control of the state so that they can use its powers for their own purposes.... Those political scientists—be they pluralist or Marxist—who try to reduce the state to being merely the operating arm of any interest group are in error.... The state has its own values, objectives and interests that cannot be reduced to those of any interest group, even one as important as business.[20]

Whatever the flaws of growth-driven politics, it is clear that such policies could not flower without the active participation of government. It is largely accepted that bureaucratic politics can play a large role in the execution of foreign policy;[21] why couldn't this happen with domestic politics? The evidence is that government in fact often organizes growth coalitions,[22] acting as the springboard for many policy initiatives.[23]

Organized interest groups—environmentalists, labor, social-issue activists—also weigh in. And also the citizens, because they vote. They do not exercise much control over business, but they do exercise some control over government, which can influence business. If wealthy interests want a large new downtown park, and the voters turn down a bond issue to pay for it, can anyone honestly conclude that the elites are running the show all the time? This happened in Seattle in the late 1990s, when the city's elite got behind a big new park, and it was squarely defeated at the polls—twice. The opposition was led by small business interests from the proposed site of the Seattle Commons park, who nonetheless were greatly outspent by supporters. It should not be mistaken for an isolated incident; in recent years Seattle voters also turned down stadium funding and rapid transit funding, and put a height limit on downtown skyscrapers, contradicting the city's elites at every turn. Rapid transit eventually was approved, but only after substantial revisions to the plan. Stadium funding eventually was secured by the legislature, but once again in much different form. And as the 1990s drew to a close, local leaders did the math and rejected efforts to support a bid for the Summer Olympics. Hardly anyone, it seemed, wanted that many people coming to Seattle, even if only to visit.

Elites are not a homogeneous monolith. Exporting industries—the real key to the economic health of any region—usually do not care about the growth machine.[24] Their interests are national and global rather than local and regional; they want mostly to be left alone (except, of course, when they consider expansion or if they fall on hard times). Of what value is it to a company, whose markets are all over the world, that developers get permits in a timely fashion, or whether shopping is done downtown or at the mall? In fact, as will be demonstrated below, the regional growth that successful export firms tend to generate can come back to haunt them.

Elites are in competition with each other, for political favors and support, for land, for customers. The tax system that advantages Boeing, for example, can hardly be said to favor relatively young industries such as software and biotechnology, and business factions within Washington State do in fact compete over that issue.

At the 1995 annual political summit of the Association of Washington Businesses, the state's largest business lobby, a panel of chief executives was asked to name the biggest issue facing each of their firms in the coming year. The answers were predictable: power prices (a utility CEO); education (a telecommunications CEO); quality of life (a high-tech CEO); business climate (a bank CEO); and state regulations (a heavy industry CEO). These are not issues that can be resolved independently. Power prices will affect the manufacturer's costs; better schools likely will mean more tax money, affecting all of the others, and especially "business climate"; quality of life is directly traceable to growth management and environmental protection and hence to regulation. Longtime state political observers say that AWB's lobbying efforts are hamstrung by the diverse constituency it serves. It cannot be strongly for anything without upsetting someone.

Why then does government persist in listening to business? As discussed above, if the economy becomes an issue, elected officials will be looking for work. Business interests can give city leaders what they want: a healthy economy (and satisfied voters), prestige, respect, and a leg up on the next election.[25]

Business attempts to legitimize its power by linking free enterprise to democracy, by using its wealth to spawn an endless media barrage that categorizes every business action as a selfless campaign for the public good. Most of the campaign is to prevent change;[26] of all the social virtues business desires, predictability must rank near the top.

Also overlooked by elite theorists are the transaction costs of political action. In assuming hegemony by elite interests, they necessarily argue that elites have power over everything that matters, at most if not at all times. But fear of public reaction is not to be ignored; why waste political capital on items of marginal interest?

The public's interest often is clearly evident on the issue of growth. The antigrowth coalition has been a significant force in Puget Sound–area politics in recent years; no-growth candidates have unseated incumbents on city and county councils and antigrowth measures have fared well at the voting booth. Antigrowth forces are not without resources; they are capable of organizing; and when it comes to voting, their members tend to outnumber the growth coalition's.

That such a coalition should arise can only complicate the competition for resources, a competition in which government is competitor, referee, and playing field. This is a relatively recent development. Examinations of the nineteenth century find great concordance between business and government.[27] The city councilmen and mayors were largely business owners, a circumstance evident elsewhere, including Seattle and its suburbs. Well into the twentieth century, the city councils of Kent, Renton, and Auburn (where Boeing would eventually become the dominant employer) were peopled by each town's leading businessmen.

Then business and government each got more complicated and time consuming. In twentieth-century America, the captains of industry were replaced by "an entirely new type: The Captains of Non-Industry, of Consumption, of Leisure," whose business interests tend to have different needs than do those of other orders.[28] When Boeing came to bat in the 1980s and 1990s, that meant it was facing government leaders who knew that business was important and why, but who knew very little about running one. They were capable of policy decisions without reference to the real cost to a business.

The other thing that happened was economic consolidation, with big firms acquiring or eclipsing smaller ones. The really large economic enterprises were increasingly absentee owned, their markets far flung, so that as long they were left alone, local politics could be of little practical interest.[29] For the upwardly mobile manager, spending much time on community activities only served to detour his career path within the corporation. Managers found that getting involved only threatened to alienate local interests, who then might cast covetous eyes on the local plant. In San Francisco, DeLeon noted that the growth coalition's demise followed a period in which business consolidation brought in more executives to San Francisco who were not from there and were less involved in city politics.[30]

Each of the models has something to offer and lessons to teach. Despite the disagreements, an impressive amount of good work has been done by researchers looking—from all angles—at community power. If there is a serious shortcoming to all this, it is that the researchers seem to have focused on what was wrong with each other's work, while missing what was good. Hence the notion of political ecology: you have to look at the whole picture. It would be foolish to study a forest ecosystem and focus only on the plants and animals while ignoring the weather and geography. And yet social science does this far too often, neglecting scientific method in favor of polemicism.

An ecological approach to political economy will look at existing social and natural structures, such as the impact of external economic conditions on political decisions. It will attempt to ignore no potential actors even as it assumes that competition between those actors will sometimes be unevenly matched. It will acknowledge that workers and capitalists may have different needs, that elites will attempt to dominate public arenas, and that groups will coalesce around issues of immediate concern. Most important, perhaps, it will not see factions as good guys or bad guys, but rather as these guys and those guys, preferring a neutral stance so as to ease the task of sorting out competing claims of civic virtue. The prudent researcher must acknowledge the tradeoffs offered and made—the opportunity cost of every public and private decision.

Let us be Marxist and elitist and pluralist: there may in fact be class-based issues at stake. There is no guarantee that the state will in fact be an independent actor. Of course there are elites; it is difficult to imagine a system without them, utopian visions about withering states and expanding souls notwithstanding. Let us also look for groups that are in competition. And let us look for groups that rise in opposition to class-based or elite maneuverings on all fronts.

An adequate model of community power must be crafted with a hard eye to the realities of local politics in their full scope. It must account for the power of elites, of government, and of other organized groups; for the role of voters; and for the sometimes competitive nature of the system. Such a view of any political system as an ecology will not be tasty to researchers who hunger for tightly drawn, compact models that sharply predict outcomes. But if anything is to be learned from the substantial work that has been done on community power, it is that Atlanta is not Detroit or New Haven or Santa Barbara. The problem with tightly drawn, compact models is that they do not translate well from one case to another in anything as messy as politics, and they miss too many things.

Let us consider this from the viewpoint of what I like to call Sell's Laws of Political Economy (which obviously borrow broadly from others' conclusions):

1. *The decision will be made in the direction of the greatest value. Usually that's money.* Governments, especially local ones, make decisions based on what is perceived to produce the most value for the community. This is not an apologia for the status quo; this is how calculations are made.

David Easton's description of politics as "the authoritative allocation of value" remains useful.[31] Easton suggests that government parcels out scarce resources based in part on various calculations of demand, supply, and worth. Consequently, business frequently will be encouraged, unless it threatens wealthy neighborhoods; a once remote sand and gravel pit now surrounded by suburbia will have a tougher time getting its operating permit renewed than will a distribution center in the midst of the industrial district. Less desirable businesses such as strip clubs will be shunted to undesirable locations. And zoning will be used to limit the percentage of apartments in a city, in part to limit the costs in city services and in part to protect the value of nearby single family homes.

This does not mean governments will not make wrong or shortsighted decisions. For example, by all accounts, urban renewal did very few favors for inner city residents in the 1960s and 1970s, and the scorecard on states' recent penchant for industrial development subsidy is incomplete. But because cities in particular have to maximize jobs, wealth, and wealthy residents—the things that pay the bills—city officials typically will move in the direction of policy that produces the greatest wealth. Nor does it mean government will always decide against environmental protection and in favor of development. In an affluent area not greatly in need of jobs, environmental concerns can and do win out. Hence my basic premise: the eternal quest for the greatest value will drive a wedge between business and government when the benefits of growth appear to be outweighed by the costs.

2. *Politics is economic competition carried on by other means.* On the other side of the equation is business, in competition with itself, with government, and with workers and consumers for a variety of scarce resources. Consequently, business interests seek to change the rules of competition through the only actor with the scope and clout to enforce such changes—government. This is evident in a variety of places, from efforts by astrologers and tattoo artists to get licensing requirements

enacted (all in the name of consumer protection, of course—and this bill has popped up more than once in the Washington State legislature) to efforts by U.S. firms to limit foreign government subsidy to foreign competitors. Marxists and various stripes of left-leaning analysts point to such efforts and conclude that markets in fact do not exist. Markets do function; firms do compete on the basis of price, quantity, and quality. But they also compete outside the market, in attempts to limit competitors' abilities to compete inside the market. As noted below, most business people favor free competition, except when it applies to them. This has been obvious at least since Adam Smith, who clearly understood that the traders and merchants of his day wanted government to restrict entry to their markets.[32]

The Second Law trades in part off Robert Leone's Iron Law of Public Policy: every government action creates winners and losers in the marketplace.[33] Wise business people know this, and act accordingly. Moreover, the domination of anything is costly, so powerful actors try to institutionalize the conditions and terms of their power.[34] Clarence N. Stone calls this "ecological power;" economists know it as market power. "Because only government combines the enforcement authority and the revenue capacity needed for genuinely broad-scale efforts, those seeking to alter the social ecology in which they operate tend to work through government."[35]

But this mechanism is as available to antigrowth forces as it is to progrowth forces. Particularly when its use hinges on elections, initiatives, and referenda, antigrowth forces may be at some advantage simply because of their greater numbers. This fact, then, becomes the hammer that drives the wedge between business and government. However much it is cloaked in the tattered cape of public policy, the competition is fundamentally economic: interest groups will seek to protect and maximize their economic returns, be it spurring economic growth or protecting quality of life.

3. *Economic interests will be politically dominant only to the extent that they are economically dominant.* The more crucial a business is to a local economy, the more it will get its way in matters of public policy. Witness Gary, Indiana's devotion to steel, or the strength of the auto industry in Michigan, or the oil industry in Texas or Alaska. The logic of this calculation is simple: if the livelihood of a region depends on a particular employer, state and local government will do what it can to keep that employer happy. The less significant the business or employer, the more difficulty it has in achieving its nonmarket ends. For example, Thomas Burke, the local lieutenant of railroad magnate James J. Hill, was a political force in Seattle in

the 1920s. It was a time when the railroad was still the best way to move goods and people long distances over land. "In Washington, railroad interests dominated the legislature as they did in other states along the northern tier. It was in these august bodies that politics blended with economics, effectively protecting advantages given to the railroads' absentee owners."[36]

But railroads are not the only ticket in town anymore. Railroads no longer own and operate the northern tier of states and California. Railroads and trucking interests have been in constant competition for decades, and the railroads' political power has waned accordingly:

> The days of states being run by one or two dominant interests ... are virtually gone. There are no longer any "company states." Many states, however, still have a single prominent interest, such as gambling in Nevada, oil in Texas, Louisiana and New Mexico; and agriculture in many farm states. But today these interests must share power with other groups. The days when one interest could dictate policy on a wide range of issues appears to be gone forever.[37]

Consequently, a once-predominant economic interest will see its political clout erode as a locality evolves and its economy diversifies. Its natural constituency—the people whose livelihoods depend directly or indirectly on its success, and who are the force that will give the economic interest victory in public policy battles—shrinks in relation to total population. This is the grease that allows the wedge to slide into and widen the gap between business and government.[38]

4. *Everyone favors economic competition, except when it applies to them.* It is a peculiarly American conceit to spout off about the virtues of the free enterprise system, and yet the history of the nation is littered with examples of people trying to get government to limit competition. And surely, one will find, when someone is losing the battle of free enterprise, the loser will begin to cry "unfair competition!" It is no accident that every state that joined in the government's antitrust case against Microsoft was home to a company competing with the software giant. Advertised as a consumer protection effort, the government's case was strangely devoid of complaints from consumers.

The relevant part of this for our purposes is that a significant chunk of the antigrowth coalition is often peopled by business owners whose livelihoods are threatened by some other firm's arrival or expansion. So what may appear on the surface to be some great concern about the environment, for example, may simply be somebody trying to preserve his or her piece of the pie. This does not necessarily make their claims less relevant or wrong, but it does categorize them as what they are.

5. *All life is politics.* This law occurred to me as the number of complaints I heard about who got hired and who got what contract began to pile up in my memory. Again, it is something of a gee-whiz notion, but it is worth repeating: people do business with the people they know. It cuts down on transaction costs; it pays psychic dividends. The lesson for relations between business and government is that successful actors on both sides will attempt to build relationships to ease the paths toward what they want, and those relationships will help ensure that they achieve their goals.

What all this adds up to for the present study is that to assume that Boeing exercises hegemony in Washington State is to miss many things. The company, as we shall see, is not part of the growth machine, and no longer occupies the dominant position it once did.

Wings of Power

BOEING AND THE POLITICS
OF GROWTH IN THE NORTHWEST

1 / The Runway

Boeing Drops a Bomb

One of the ironies of history is the tendency toward contradiction....
A social or historical contradiction involves producing the means of its
destruction or transformation to its opposite, simultaneously with (and
as an integral part of) producing an intended achievement. The more
people, institutions or entire political economies succeed in achieving
desired goals, in other words, the more that very success produces resistance or other forces or conditions that threaten to transform such
achievements into their opposite.
—Kenneth M. Dolbeare, 1988

FRANK SHRONTZ is not, at first glance, a remarkable man. His well-cut suits
would set him apart as a person of above-average but not ostentatious taste
and means; the warm confidence of his gaze and slight smile might suggest
a certain degree of happiness. Before his retirement in 1996, his speech in
public tended to be measured and restrained. At press conferences he often
seemed to be bemused by all the attention. Before he became the chairman
and chief executive officer of the Boeing Company, neighbors knew him as
a guy who got more barbecue sauce on his apron than on the steaks. Near
the end of his tenure as head of the world's largest commercial aerospace
firm, in 1996, Shrontz admitted that, at heart, he was still a kid from Idaho.

But a very successful and important one. It was Shrontz who, earlier in
his career, got Boeing market forecasters to tweak projected sales numbers
a bit for a new version of the 737, helping to convince Boeing's board to
OK the project. It went on to become the world's best-selling jetliner. Ele-
vated to CEO in 1985 and chairman in 1987, Shrontz helped guide Boeing to
undisputed status as the world's number one commercial aerospace firm.
Boeing sales and employment climbed, and its new 777 model, by the early

1990s, promised to be one of the company's most successful products ever. Sales had risen from $16.3 billion in Shrontz's first year as chairman to $29.3 billion in 1991, with profits climbing from $665 million to $1.5 billion.

Shrontz was tabbed to be the keynote speaker for the Greater Seattle Chamber of Commerce's annual luncheon on September 20, 1991, where he was introduced by Seattle Mayor Norm Rice. "When we think of Boeing, we think of a company that has risen to the pinnacle of success despite stiff competition," Rice said. "We also think of a company that has given back to its community," he added, citing a recent national United Way award for Boeing, and its support for education and the arts. Because he was following 1990 keynoter Bill Gates (the founder of Microsoft), Shrontz, then sixty-one, quipped, "I'm glad to see the chamber is continuing its tradition of bringing in successful, brilliant young men to speak."

Shrontz showed a Boeing-produced video about what the company was up to as it headed toward a record year for sales and profits. He praised the area for its work ethic and for its strong political leadership. And he talked about the company's future. Amid those comments, he dropped a bomb: Boeing was unhappy with the cost of doing business in Washington State. Given the choice, it would seriously consider producing its next product somewhere other than hard by the shores of Puget Sound. "It takes us as long to get a permit here as it does to build and design a new airplane," Shrontz said, citing the nearly $50 million the City of Everett wanted as mitigation for expansion of its plant there.

In a press conference following, Shrontz reiterated his comments. "We have some concerns about the time that it takes for us to build new facilities and the cost of building them. For future expansion we're going to have to look elsewhere for alternatives," he said. "If the rates of increase and costs of doing business here don't come down, it's unlikely we'll increase our presence here."

Shrontz cautioned that Boeing was not flying away. "Short of a major downturn in the market or other considerations, we do not intend to pack up and go anywhere," he said. But the company had decided to build its new wind tunnel out of state, concerned about what it would cost to get through the local process. "Could Puget Sound turn into an aerospace rust belt in the 21st century, complete with padlocked factories, unemployment lines and urban blight? It certainly could."[1]

The timing of Shrontz's speech lent more than a little drama to the proceedings. It was becoming apparent by then that the aerospace business cycle was about to ebb and that Boeing employment was likely to fall. That in itself is usually enough to send ripples of worry across Puget Sound. Anyone who had lived in the area for any length of time knew that as Boeing went, so went the region's economy. "When Boeing gets the sniffles, Seattle catches a cold," was the common refrain.

But as the region had grown, it had wrestled with the other side of growth—gridlocked traffic, soaring real estate prices, increasing pollution, urban sprawl, and loss of green space—and with the social and economic costs of that growth. Antigrowth forces had been rising for years, landing so-called slow-growth advocates in state and local offices, turning back progrowth initiatives, and even going so far as to put a lid on the height of buildings in downtown Seattle.

Despite all its success, Boeing appeared to be in the fight of its life against the feisty Airbus consortium of Europe. Airbus had all but put McDonnell Douglas out of the commercial jetliner business and had loudly announced that its goal was no longer 30 percent of the market, but 50 percent. Some of that pie would have to be sliced off Boeing's piece for that to happen. Airbus trumpeted its products as technologically superior to Boeing's, but the real fear in Boeing's offices was that the company would be unable to compete with the substantial government subsidy Airbus had used to survive and grow. While working the political side of that contest in Washington, D.C., at home Boeing was becoming increasingly focused on keeping costs and the time it took to do things as small as possible.

So Shrontz's speech was shocking news in a region where Boeing had long been not just an employer but a way of life. By this point Boeing engineers and machinists could talk about when their grandparents had worked for the company. The professional basketball team, the Super Sonics, had been named for the ill-fated SST. In the town where the world's biggest jets were built in the world's biggest building, Boeing was an employer, and also a point of civic pride.

Shrontz's bombshell sent into flight an ample flock of hand-wringing and second-guessing. In Renton and Everett, city officials who had only recently argued about why they were not getting more money from Boeing began to back-pedal, at least verbally. The Renton City Council went so far as to pass a resolution vowing to help Boeing however it could, and the Port of Seattle invited Boeing to have a look at its land portfolio to see if anything was to its liking. Within months, Democrat Governor Mike Lowry had convened a blue-ribbon commission on regulatory reform.

It might be tempting to conclude that the story stops there, Boeing and government having proved that big business (in political science jargon, the so-called elite actors) is uncommonly and unhealthily dominant in American politics, especially at the local level. Of course, the story is more complicated than that, and the ending no more clear than a typical gray day in Seattle.

Have no doubt: Boeing is a big company, and a big presence in Seattle and the world. Although at times Boeing is bashed for the troubles it has in increasing production rates (in the late 1980s and again in the mid-1990s, for example), at other times it is freely mentioned in the same sentences as other giants of U.S. business. It is the world's largest builder of commercial jet transports, the world's largest aerospace firm, and the leading exporter in the United States. At a time when 60 to 70 percent of Boeing's sales in any given year might go overseas, a few extra deliveries can make the nation's trade balance look tolerable or ugly. It is no accident that Seattle and Boeing got so many visits and such support from the Clinton administration. Some two-thirds of the money lent by the Export-Import Bank goes to Boeing, which, in good times, is regularly cited as one of the best and most-admired U.S. corporations.

Commercial aerospace is a viciously cyclical business, where airlines seem to regularly binge and purge when it comes to ordering jetliners. Airplane companies sometimes go a full year without booking a single order, then soon after land hundreds of orders in the same space of time. Despite this, Boeing has been profitable since the 1950s (1997 being the sole exception; operating profits remained solid, but the company took huge write-offs to cover the cost of fixing its production problems). Boeing has built 60 percent of the jetliners ever flown and is the only company to be consistently profitable at that business. It built the first successful jet transport, the 707, and the largest, the 747. It remained profitable throughout the early 1990s, a time when its customers, the world's airlines, were losing more money than they had made in the industry's entire history. Paying close attention to the travel business and its customers' needs, Boeing regularly bets the company on multi-billion-dollar projects which, so far, have paid off.

Prior to its merger with McDonnell Douglas in 1997, Boeing had plants in eleven states and three countries. But its headquarters, the bulk of its operations, and its heart and soul were (and are) in the Seattle area. Since World War II, it has been the single largest private employer in the state, and the largest employer in the Seattle metropolitan area, with a local payroll of as many as 100,000 at any one time. Its output represents, by one estimate, 18 percent of the state's gross domestic product and 17 percent of its total personal income. According to that study, by a trio of respected Seattle-area economists, despite the great diversification of the non-aerospace economy, Boeing's economic impact was as great in 1990 as it was twenty or thirty years before, before Microsoft and biotechnology and everything else that has followed. They calculated that 389,000 jobs in the state are related to Boeing, figuring that each Boeing job is worth 2.8 jobs elsewhere in the economy.[2]

The assumption among many outside observers is that this economic impact and community stature translate into political power. In her research on state-level interest groups, Sarah McCally Morehouse decided that Boeing was the most influential lobbyist in Washington State.[3] Consider as well this passage from *The Economist*, tossed off with its usual glib abandon:

> In 75 years Boeing has become the largest aerospace company in the world and has come to influence daily life in its home state of Washington—economically, politically, culturally—on a scale unmatched by any other firm in America.... Few bills pass the state Legislature without Boeing's stamp of approval. A proposal this year that Boeing pay $300 million sales tax on its imports was savagely attacked. Environmental and trade union bills also come under critical scrutiny from Boeing lobbyists.[4]

By the time that was written, however, the state legislature had passed the Growth Management Act, which Boeing didn't support and was already much regretting. (And it was, ultimately, the GMA that provided the fuel for Shrontz's speech.) For all the things it already had—a favorable tax structure, an educational system pointed in its direction, reasonably good labor relations, and its own workers compensation plan—Boeing in the 1990s was finding it very difficult to get anything more.

Although it successfully stalled the City of Seattle for years as the city tried to annex more of that precious Duwamish Basin industrial land, it still could not prevent a city official from stalling a building permit for three costly weeks. He had, it seems, locked it in his desk and gone away on vacation. And although Boeing clearly is the dominant employer in Renton and Everett, it could not dodge $49 million in impact fees levied by the two cities (for transportation and other infrastructure improvements). This came at a time when other local governments around the country were offering and spending that kind of money to lure businesses their way. And, as we shall see, all of Boeing's complaints about the miasma of environmental and growth-management laws could not pry much action out of a legislature that was otherwise bent on property rights reform.

The genesis of this story derives in part from the peculiar politics and geography of Seattle and Washington State. But it also reveals a new stage in the evolution of the American political economy. Throughout most of American history, business and government have gotten along. Usually, they have worked together, with government seeking to create the conditions that allow economic success, while business repays the favor by providing jobs and tax revenue. This completely symbiotic relationship describes most of what has happened throughout U.S. history.

But things change. Some combination of relative prosperity and urban in-fill will alter the business-government equation enough to disrupt the traditional concordance that the two sides have enjoyed, at least since the Founding Fathers made property rights one of their chief concerns. Growth drives a wedge between the groups that often make up what many researchers have called "the growth coalition." While business and government usually march hand in hand in support of economic development, if they are successful enough, that partnership will fray if not unravel, undone by the weight of its success.

The reason for this is a form of the law of diminishing marginal returns, but let's call it the Paradox of Growth. Growth eventually produces conditions that hinder further growth—rising land prices, pollution, too much traffic, excessive strains on infrastructure and the general quality of life. This erodes the benefits that growth originally produced—jobs, money, a greater community sense of well-being. The public response to growth-related problems can eventually reverse the very growth the community once sought to generate as businesses leave for areas with lower costs and better quality of life. Economic expansion, checked or unchained, eventually ensures its own decay.

Whereas economic growth usually is the primary goal of local business and political leaders, eventually, diminishing marginal returns will set in. Growth is initially favored because it generates jobs, which boost tax revenue, decrease social welfare expenditures, raise living standards, and increase social stability. But growth also generates externalities, unintended costs that are borne both by governments and their constituents: traffic congestion; pollution; urban/suburban sprawl and attendant loss of open, undeveloped, and green space; rising housing prices; and increasing demands on all sorts of public facilities and services. Ostensibly, growth should pay for itself, but governments in fact have a limited ability to capture revenues from growth, especially when inflation is factored in. Income and property taxes may provide some protection against inflation, rising as incomes and property values rise, but consumption taxes are particularly vulnerable to erosion. (Rising prices, for example, can decrease consumption, with tax revenues falling in step. Even if revenues remain stable, however, inflation will increase the costs of goods and services that government must purchase.) As any investor knows, even moderate inflation can erode the returns on fixed-income assets, driving investors and governments to seek returns that outstrip inflation. Governments run the risk of voter and business disapproval when they raise taxes, however, and so lack a free hand to raise money to accommodate the growth they so often pursue. (At one point in the 1980s, Houston, surely a progrowth city in a progrowth state, went so far as to ask businesses to locate outside of the city because the city could no longer provide or support the infrastructure that more growth demanded.)[5]

When the costs of growth begin to outweigh the benefits, the usual coalition that favors growth may splinter, or, at a minimum, face serious opposition from groups whose livelihoods do not depend on growth and whose quality of life is threatened by it. Whereas most urban communities now sport "sensible growth" advocates, it is in those places where growth causes more problems than it solves that those advocates succeed.

Business, which plays an important though not exclusive role in generating economic growth, is consequently faced with what looks to it like a two-pronged assault. On the one hand, it faces higher taxes; on the other, it confronts potentially powerful adversaries who want to reduce its decision-making power and to block further growth, which may affect its ability to do business. As a consequence, as has been seen in New York and California, business sometimes relocates rather than fight such battles.

It is a tertiary stage in American political economy. In the initial stage, from the Revolution through the nineteenth century, business was government and vice versa. The city council was likely to be peopled with a community's top business leaders. Given the largely hands-off nature of government's attitude toward business, it was not likely the two parties would find much to disagree on. In the second stage, beginning roughly with the first half of the twentieth century, business got bigger and more complicated, and the business people who still got really involved in politics were not the big players. But government's role in the economy was still so small as to leave little chance for serious conflict. In the third stage, which began to show up in California and New York in the 1960s, government got a whole lot bigger even as business became more complicated and time-consuming. Government became a profession unto itself, featuring full-time city and county councils and legislatures filled with people who not only did not own businesses, but who often had not worked much in the private sector before entering public life.

Hence the Paradox of Growth. Observers as diverse as Jürgen Habermas and Daniel Patrick Moynihan have said as much.[6] In a speech to a group of business executives, Moynihan put it succinctly: "As capitalism succeeds, as people in general get to be pretty well off, more and more of them evolve life-styles that are basically normative.... So the success of capitalism is doing what Schumpeter predicted: It is increasingly diminishing the capitalist's function in the system."[7]

Even more directly, Theodore J. Lowi dissected the entrails of this dilemma only a few years later:

> Popular rule was all right so long as popular institutions chose to do nothing. As soon as state assemblies and Congress became captured by majorities favorable to regular and frequent state intervention, the inconsistencies between the demands of capitalist ideology and the demands of popular-rule ideology became clear.[8]

Even that might not have produced discordance except for the issue of growth. Especially in California, and more recently in Western Washington and Oregon, but also in other large urban and land-constrained areas, the Paradox of Growth began to raise quality-of-life issues that disrupted the previously relentless drive of the "growth coalition."[9] This combination of such elements as realtors, developers, retailers, and media outlets, the people who stand to benefit the most from continuing growth, suddenly finds opposition to what heretofore had been a universally good idea: let's make the community grow.

Such growth occurred in the Puget Sound area over the fifty years of Boeing's rise to aerospace dominance, and it seems to have affected the company in two ways. First, Boeing's growth helped generate the region's growth, which served to raise the issue of growth itself: How much can we afford? When is bigger not better? Second, the surplus wealth that Boeing produced helped spawn economic diversification, so that there were Seattle people whose daily lives did not appear to cross paths with Boeing's, people whose jobs did not depend on aerospace (regardless of what they say in *The Economist*). Remember Sell's Third Law: *Economic interests will be politically dominant only to the extent that they are economically dominant.* And although the Pascall, Pedersen, and Conway study showed Boeing is still the wind beneath Seattle's wings, the public perception may not be the same. When such a perception changes, the wishes of any one economic sector will carry less weight, both among the public and among policy makers.

This is not a theory for all times and all places; if anything, the study of politics should tell the observer that life is a pretty complicated thing, and the saga of Seattle might never repeat as the woe of Wichita (where Boeing also has long been a big employer). But it may suggest patterns that will repeat themselves in cities that outgrow their comfort levels.

2 / Come Fly with Us

A Short History of Boeing and Seattle

There is not much to that machine of Maroney's. I think we could build a better one.

—William E. Boeing, circa 1914

Driving in a loop around Seattle and its suburbs, you rarely see a clear patch of sky unoccupied by airplanes.

—Karl Sabbagh, 1996

THE HISTORY of The Boeing Company is regaled in varying detail in a hangarful of sanitized recitations, from Boeing public relations director Harold Mansfield's *Vision* to Robert Serling's company-sponsored *Legend and Legacy* (Eugene Rodgers's *Flying High* is a notable exception). Even less benign examinations, such as John Newhouse's *The Sporty Game*, have not really understood the company; Newhouse, for example, smugly predicted that the 737 would be lucky to equal the success of the 727, which ended production with close to 2,000 orders. The 737, now by far the world's best-selling jetliner, has had more than 3,000 orders and recently underwent a serious redesign that should keep it aloft for some time to come.

Boeing, the company, came to Seattle by chance. Boeing, the founder, did not. His father was in the timber and mining business, and long before Washington State had airplanes, it had trees. William E. Boeing was born in Detroit on October 1, 1881. His father died when the younger Boeing was eight. He attended school in Switzerland and then studied engineering at Yale, dropping out of that institution (thus starting a line of prominent Northwesterners who were Ivy League dropouts and who went on to fame and fortune. See Gates, Bill.)

Boeing did not trust his stepfather, and set off to secure his own fortune.[1] That landed him in Aberdeen, Washington, on the Pacific Coast, in 1903, where his father had already made large land acquisitions. (Grays Harbor County also lent another famous son to aviation, Reuben Fleet, founder of Consolidated Aircraft, later a part of General Dynamics.) An Aberdeen logger who knew him described young Boeing as a "real Grays Harbor citizen, a real logger and a real man."[2]

Boeing's holdings were large, and he knew enough to run a sawmill and make money. Money took him to Seattle in 1908, and to Los Angeles, on a visit, in January 1910. It was then that the most important airplane ride in the history of commercial aviation did not happen. William E. Boeing, twenty-eight, lumber lama and timber tycoon, watched a French aviator push his primitive plane around the field at an air show in Los Angeles. For three days thereafter, Boeing tried unsuccessfully to get a ride. Eventually, the French pilot packed up his plane and went home, no doubt leaving young Boeing with the taste of anticipation still fresh on his tongue.[3] Back in Seattle, in October 1913, members at the University Club teased Boeing about his interest in airplanes. He predicted that someday aircraft would make regular passenger flights, like trains. This got even more laughter.[4]

Boeing got his plane ride in Seattle in 1914, when a barnstormer named Terah Maroney visited town with his seaplane. In tow was Boeing's chum, U.S. Navy officer G. Conrad Westervelt, whose initial association with Boeing and subsequent transfer to duty on the East Coast sort of makes him the Wally Pipp of aviation. Boeing was hooked on flying and bought a Martin seaplane and flying lessons in 1915. Some histories say Boeing crashed his Martin in Lake Washington, but the pilot and mechanic Herb Munter later confessed to the sin.[5] Impatient for the repair of the aircraft, Boeing decided to build his own.[6]

Boeing, Westervelt, and Munter set out to build airplanes. Boeing had taken his yacht for work at the Heath Shipyards, then bought the place for "$10 and considerations" when it went bankrupt.[7] The shipyard, on the banks of the Duwamish River, was to be the start of the Boeing Company; it was there that Pacific Aero Products, incorporated with $100,000 and an idea, began its operation in 1916. Boeing hoped to sell his B&W seaplane to the U.S. Navy. It was a lot like the Martin, but with lighter pontoons and better wings. Wings—and the engineering that went into them—were to become a hallmark of the company.

Boeing set out with the intention of making the airplane more than a curiosity. The Wright brothers, for instance, could not get any reporters on site to witness their historic first flight, and few papers reported the event. The U.S. Army originally could see no use for aircraft, even after the Wrights' historic first flight. Just months before the flight, a respected American scientist had published a paper proving that powered heavier-than-air flight was impossible.[8]

Boeing went so far as to take his plane aloft and bomb Seattle with red cardboard shells, extolling the virtues and importance of aircraft: "For our national defense, encourage aviation ... for our country needs more airplanes."[9] World War I made that true. The war was a boon for Pacific Aero, reconfigured as the Boeing Airplane Company in 1918. By 1919 Boeing had an office in Washington, D.C., seeking airplane contracts with the Navy.

After the war, however, things got very thin. Ninety percent of the nation's aviation firms went out of business. Boeing survived by building bedroom furniture and fast boats, and because its owner had extraordinarily deep pockets. And as Rodgers aptly notes, unlike the founders of virtually every other airplane company, Bill Boeing was a businessman, not a fly boy.[10]

There was nothing about the Northwest that should have lent itself to aviation. Unlike California, the region made no effort to attract defense or aviation interests.[11] Boeing succeeded in part because William E. Boeing could afford to meet the payroll when things were tight, in part because he owned vast tracts of spruce, the key ingredient in early aircraft frames, and in part because he placed a strong and early emphasis on engineering.

Perhaps the key variable was the price-to-weight ratio of the product. Airplanes come with shipping included:

> Manufacturing industries tend to develop near the market for their output. For any factor of production to attract a manufacturing operation at a distance from its market, the economies which result must exceed the savings in transportation costs which would follow from a location at the market. Resources, especially raw materials, and labor are the chief factors of production to outweigh this powerful pull of markets.[12]

And so the wealth of trees allowed the development of a new industry, much as the wealth of aircraft would later seed new industries in the decades to come. Seattle had the basics—enough size to provide electrical power to run a factory; a university to provide skilled engineers; enough population to provide a labor pool; and rail and water access to allow the import of parts, especially engines.

Seattle was a young but growing town when Bill Boeing arrived. It was founded by the ancestors of the growth coalition; when the Denny Party arrived in 1851 they had in mind commerce, not farming.[13] That Washington is the most trade dependent state in the nation should be of no surprise; from the start, the city was so far from everything else that trade was the only way to make a living.

It was always a region of deceptive wealth. Before "the Boston men" came, it was home to a rich and diverse Native American culture, grown wealthy on a moderate climate and rivers and bays filled with salmon and shellfish. Its tall stands of timber gave the first white settlers something to sell to the first San Francisco packet that came looking for pilings; its coal brought legions of immigrants who put down roots and built the towns where Boeing would later build plants. The Green River Valley, eventually home to 40,000 Boeing workers, was, in the 1890s, the hops-growing capital of the world. People could make money in Seattle, and they did. One of those people was Bill Boeing, whose company proceeded to prosper in a business where most would crash and burn.

The city that made this possible grew not so much because of what was there as because of what was near. "The first in Washington's series of economic booms (always, it seems, followed by comparable depressions) began with the discovery of gold in Alaska in 1897."[14] Seattle staked its claim as the chief shipping point to Alaska, a distinction it still holds. The city's population soared from 1,100 in 1870 to 42,000 in 1890 and to 237,000 in 1910,[15] with the biggest spurt coming in the Gold Rush decade, 1900–1910. Statewide, it was the largest relative population gain in Washington's history, and Seattle grew the most.[16] (It might have grown even more without the burden of railroader James J. Hill's monopolistic, gouging practices.[17] As in many other western states, railroads dominated Washington politics for decades.)[18] By 1910, the state was more than half urban.[19]

Edwin J. Cohn, Jr., concludes that there was no particular reason why Seattle developed ahead of its neighbors on Puget Sound, also blessed with fine natural harbors. "The best explanation of Seattle's capture of the Alaska trade and consequent spectacular growth is that a few of its citizens were particularly aggressive and imaginative."[20] The real coup was getting the federal government to put an assay office in Seattle, because anyone who actually found gold had to go to Seattle to stake a claim.[21]

Aside from shipyards, Boeing was the city's first manufacturer of any consequence. As early as 1928, Boeing was the Seattle area's largest industrial employer, even with only 900 workers. Statewide, Boeing was not the story it was to become, however: two-thirds of the state's jobs were timber-related, and Washington was the leading lumber-producing state in the country.[22] But the company's position in the local community already was substantial.

Sixty-three years later, Shrontz's 1991 speech was clearly a practice drone, an unmanned aircraft sent up to draw fire. The handful of reporters in attendance, broadcast and print, all loaded, aimed, and blazed away. None of those present—myself included—had any sense of history. As it turns out, Boeing has been threatening to leave Seattle for one reason or another almost from the start. (We also proved, once again, that journalists can write but not read; only two years before, a nationwide poll of business executives said Seattle had the best business climate in the United States.[23] If the climate was so good, why was Boeing so anxious to leave?)

In 1921, Boeing asked the Seattle Chamber of Commerce to pressure the city to extend utilities to its Duwamish manufacturing site, then outside the city limits, to speed up road projects, and to get federal funding to put a bridge across the Duwamish. Or it would move to Los Angeles. By 1922, the improvements were made. The company soon had authority to dictate conditions at nearby King County Airport—now better known as Boeing Field—and it ordered "the Rushlite-Gray Aviation Co. to move its airplanes from the field."[24]

As a successful company, Boeing was soon being courted by other cities, including Portland and San Francisco. Boeing once had some southern California operations, "but did not find its natural advantages sufficiently compelling to stay there."[25] But Boeing never hesitated to use such leverage against both the area and its workers.

> Boeing management, striking a pose that would become familiar in the years ahead, declared: "The attitude of organized labor ... must be weighed as one of the major factors by the company, in considering [these] overtures.... Because of the difference between wage rates which Boeing has paid and those of competitive factories, the company has remained in Seattle only with difficulty. [Its] market is a national or world market.... This is what governs allowable production costs."[26]

With slight alteration, any Boeing executive could have given that speech today and not been out of place; many have.

And yet the area always appeared to have been bent on helping Boeing succeed. When it needed land for expanded production in the 1930s, farmer Guiseppe Desimone sold the company forty acres of Duwamish land for one dollar, in part because he could afford it and in part because he liked the company. Boeing, as usual, was making noises about leaving.[27]

But Boeing stayed and, like Seattle, weathered its own series of booms and busts. The company's early contracts were mostly military, from re-modeling old de Havillands to building an odd assortment of aircraft for the Army and Navy. Aside from underbidding its competitors thanks to Boeing's spruce, the small company also learned to do more with less and generally needed fewer man-hours to build an airplane than did its competitors. Early on it established the hallmarks of its later operations, such as asking customers what they wanted and then betting the store on building the right product for the right market.

James C. Collins and Jerry I. Porras concluded that Boeing succeeded so well for so long because the company had a vision of more than just profit, and that it was willing to take gambles.[28] Boeing's record of firsts stretches throughout the company's history, from the first metal fuselage to the first all-metal airplane; the first retractable landing gear; the first pressurized cabin; the first four-engine bomber; the first international mail flight; the first successful commercial jet transport (the first jet transport, the British Comet, had the unseemly habit of exploding in mid-flight); to such space-breaking products as the Saturn V rocket booster and the Lunar Rover. When Franklin Roosevelt became the first president to fly, he was aboard a Boeing Clipper. Boeing's airline operations were the first to use flight attendants, and the company was probably the first to hire Asian Americans and women as engineers.[29] (It did not hire African Americans until World War II all but forced the issue, and the company's largest union battled internally about that question for years. The Machinists Union admitted women as members only under pressure from the government during the war, and refused to admit any people of color until 1948.)[30]

Boeing first sold stock to the public in 1928. In 1929, Bill Boeing renamed his creation United Aircraft & Transportation, which included Boeing, United Air Lines, Hamilton Standard, Northrop, Pratt & Whitney, Sikorsky, Stearman, Chance Vought, two other airlines, an airport management company, and a flight school. It had won several lucrative U.S. airmail contracts, and its Model 247 airliner was the class of the sky. The horizon showed nothing but sunshine, but two things happened to change everything.

First, and largely overlooked by most historians,[31] was that by giving United Air Lines a two-year exclusive lead on the 247, it prompted other airlines to pressure Douglas Aircraft into building the DC-3. The benefit of coming in second in the rapidly changing world of aerospace is that it affords a chance to improve on the winning design, and the DC-3 was better than the 247—it was faster and it carried more people. Douglas eventually sold about 3,000 of them, a record not surpassed until the maturity of the 737. Boeing never signed a deal like that again.

Second, in 1934 Congress passed the U.S. Air Mail Act, an antitrust bill forbidding the same company from building airplanes and carrying the mail, which resulted in the breakup of United Aircraft & Transportation. Boeing and other firms were caught amid some scandal, the result of the postmaster general having divided up the profitable mail routes among the nation's fledgling airlines (thus further reducing the competition he was supposed to create).[32] A frustrated Bill Boeing, who had officially retired at age fifty the year before,[33] sold his stock and walked away, having only rare and marginal contact with his creation ever after.[34] Despite Bill Boeing, Jr.'s later passion for Republican causes,[35] a potential family dynasty passed away prematurely, which altered the equation of Boeing's political power in untold ways.

The Boeing Airplane Company was the smallest piece of what was left. Its pre-break-up management remained in charge. Only the company's attention to engineering excellence and customer service kept it alive until World War II. Throughout most of the 1930s, it was a distant third in the commercial aviation business.

World War II kept Boeing afloat just as World War I had. It also taught the company something about mass production and efficiency. Boeing factories rolled out thousands of planes for the war, and made the company whole and healthy once more. The federal Defense Plant Corporation helped Boeing build big new factories in Seattle and Renton,[36] and federal dollars helped provide the company with sophisticated aeronautical research capability.[37] The war boosted the company into the big time, and it permanently altered the landscape.[38]

This was when Boeing really began to have an impact on the community. Before the war, Seattle really was not dependent on Boeing; Richard S. Kirkendall notes the importance of the shipyards and says it was more of a Navy town. After World War I, for example, U.S. Senator Homer Bone, one of the state's more prominent intrawar politicians, once attacked William Boeing on the floor of the U.S. Senate for war profiteering, drawing little if any protest from home.[39] Ironically, Bone was a champion of public power, which made electricity cheap (published plans by private power companies for tapping the energy wealth of the Columbia River system included such ideas as building a canal from the Columbia River to Spokane, and putting a dam on the canal). Cheap electricity made the Northwest's now substantial aluminum industry possible—two factors that helped keep Boeing in Seattle. It takes extraordinary amounts of electricity to separate alumina from bauxite ore, and hydroelectric dams make that possible. And most of the aluminum was going to Boeing.[40]

By 1943, Boeing contracts for military planes totaled $1 billion, nearly double the value of the state's total manufacturing output in 1939. Aircraft manufacturing space went from 800,000 square feet to 4.1 million square feet; Boeing employment rose from 7,500 in 1940 to 32,000 in 1943, including 10,000 in Renton. King County population grew by 100,000 in two years, and Renton's population tripled. Aluminum production went from zero before the war to one-third of the nation's total output.[41] By 1944, Boeing had 50,000 employees in the area and $600 million in sales, or 10 times the value of Seattle's manufacturing output in 1939.[42] During the war, Boeing also had parts facilities across the state, in Aberdeen, Bellingham, Hoquiam, Everett, and Chehalis, and two in Tacoma,[43] along with 67 subcontractors in the state.[44] "More than most aircraft manufacturers, Boeing engaged in extensive subcontracting, building an intricate network throughout the west," Gerald D. Nash noted. "It built an intricate feeder network of thousands of small shops in the Pacific Northwest."[45] It had thirty-six major local subcontractors, all still in business by 1950. Four of those firms were "war babies," started just to supply defense firms during the war.[46]

The impact on the Seattle area was substantial. By the end of World War II, one in six people in King County worked at Boeing.[47] Boeing's employment needs were so great that the federal government apparently got workers moved from the shipyards to Boeing and canceled some contracts with small firms to encourage workers to move to Boeing.[48] The county's population grew from 504,000 in 1940 to 732,992 in 1950.[49] Foreshadowing what was to come in the 1980s and 1990s, growth-related problems sprouted as soon as the wartime boom began—housing shortages, rising crime, fire hazards, public health issues, overcrowded schools, and overburdened roads.[50] The end of the war brought a lot of change in a hurry. "For Washington state's economy, World War II ended and the postwar era began not at Hiroshima or Nagasaki or aboard the battleship Missouri, but in the board room at the Boeing Company. The date was September 5, 1945."[51] It was then that William Allen, a relatively young attorney, was chosen as Boeing's new CEO, and it was Allen who guided the company into the jet age. Among Allen's earliest moves was to respond to a huge cancellation of government orders by slashing 20,000 jobs.[52]

Boeing's continued survival was no sure thing. Although it had ranked twelfth among the nation's wartime contractors, it was no better than fifth among wartime aircraft suppliers.[53] Sales in the first peacetime year fell to $14 million, and employment fell to 11,000. The state's congressional delegation moved to try to protect aero jobs. The mayor of Seattle, business leaders, and union officials all pitched in to lobby Congress, and downtown Seattle witnessed a massive pro-Boeing rally. "Many people now considered Boeing's economic health essential to Seattle's welfare. Support for the company ran across class lines."[54] Nothing worked. Employment slipped to 9,000, and the Renton plant was closed. In 1946, Boeing actually posted a loss.[55]

But help was on the way from varied sources. Boeing and other aircraft firms lobbied the government to do something to preserve the capability that had been developed during the war.[56] Buoyed by the success of the B-17, the U.S. Army Air Corps linked its fortunes to Boeing in hopes of getting both funding and independence. Eventually they succeeded, and the war experience gave the company a big political ally in the shiny new Air Force. But that was not all.

> Furthermore, the company now had another ally willing to enter the political arena on its behalf. This was Seattle. The people there had a new commitment to Boeing. Taking advantage of cold war fears, Air Force leaders lobbied for funds to be spent on bombers, and Seattle people worked to draw that money to their city by way of Boeing.[57]

Nonetheless, in 1948, Boeing moved some of its military production to Wichita, sending shivers down the region's fiscal spine. It had already built a large satellite facility there during the war to crank out B-17s and B-29s.[58] It was a watershed event in the public mind, but was, in actuality, of only limited significance. Rival unionists used it to accuse each other of goofing things up. In Seattle, they worried that Boeing was leaving for good, and in Renton, "Boeing is shutting this down and moving it to Wichita" has ever since been the second most commonly uttered phrase after "Hello." (While covering Boeing for *Valley Daily News* in Renton, over the course of four years I got a call on this rumor at least once every couple of months.)

Boeing actually moved military production to Wichita, long the home of its Stearman division, largely in response to federal pressure; the military was concerned about having nearly all of its aircraft plants on the West Coast. All the California firms also opened plants farther east about the same time.[59] But none of them packed up and left the coast completely, either.

Robert J. Serling writes that William Allen faced considerable pressure to move the company elsewhere.[60] But apparently he recognized, as others have since, that Boeing's Seattle-area work force probably would not move to Wichita, or anywhere else.

> Meanwhile, a corps of specialized engineering talent and technical skill was being trained. It is this induced locational force, rather than any original factor, which appears to have been primarily responsible for keeping Boeing in Seattle.... Persistent rumors that Boeing was about to move completely to Wichita, Kansas, less exposed to air attack than Puget Sound, have caused consternation in Seattle and led to the launching of "Save Boeing" campaigns. At present, despite the disadvantages, both economic and military, there appears little prospect of a complete shift.[61]

Allen was in fact unhappy at having to make the move,[62] and Boeing officials said as much in public. "A community economy has been built up around these plants, and thousands of workers, many owning their own homes, have established themselves near them," said Executive Vice-President Wellwood Beall. "The people of the west coast would probably elect not to change their location."[63] Seattle and the region chipped in to ensure that more of Boeing would not go east, including the state's congressional delegation, Governor Arthur B. Langlie, the Seattle Chamber of Commerce (which launched the Save Boeing Committee), and even representatives from outlying areas of the state. The pressure campaign eventually elicited a promise from the federal government that it would not make Boeing move entirely and would send enough work Boeing's way to keep employment at prewar levels.[64]

In the midst of all this, Boeing had to sort out its relationship with its employees, a large number of whom were and are represented by District Lodge 751 of the International Association of Machinists and Aerospace Workers. The birth and early life of Boeing's largest union was, at times, as rancorous as that of any major industrial union. At other times, however, it was benign, which in part explains the relative peace eventually enjoyed by employer and employees at Boeing. The IAM's Seattle chapter was founded in 1935, actually invited in by the company so as to avoid more radical union groups.[65] At first, the company and the union enjoyed good relations. John McCann writes that the War Labor Board's policies and the company's growth worked to change that. Ultimately, Boeing's top manager very nearly succeeded in creating real animosity between the company and its workers.[66]

While California firms such as Lockheed and Douglas spent the intrawar and early World War II years doing anything to crush unionism, at Boeing "relatively high wages, factionalism and federally aided repression prevented its transformation into militancy."[67] But disagreements over wages and seniority led to a strike in April 1948. The company, as usual, threatened to leave the area if the union did not behave; the Machinists said Boeing was hurting the region by refusing to negotiate and get its employees back to work.[68] On one side were the Machinists, on the other, Boeing CEO William Allen. McCann writes that Allen "brought a lawyer's mind to the job. He also brought a certain legalistic meanness, an attention to the contract and to legality, and a disregard for the worker except as an instrument in the process of production."[69]

Allen wanted a different union, the Teamsters, whose local leader, Dave Beck, was against strikes. Beck was more than happy to step in, saying the strike would hurt Seattle and drive Boeing off to Wichita.[70] Although Beck scared some business people, those who knew him liked him, for, as Murray Morgan has noted, Beck was essentially one of them.[71] The strike dragged on for five months before the Machinists went back to work. They were nudged by the government, which was concerned about military production as the Cold War heated up. But in November 1948, the Fighting Machinists, as they sometimes like to be known, easily defeated the Teamsters in a union representation election and began to get what they wanted at the bargaining table.[72]

Allen was not done, however. In 1956 he supported Initiative 158, the first of two right-to-work measures pushed by the Boeing Company. McCann writes that the Machinists' opposition to I-158 was "crucial," and they managed to get the governor and the state's two U.S. senators (all Democrats) to come out against the measure.[73] I-158 was defeated soundly at the polls. Allen pushed the right-to-work I-202 in 1958, even trying to get supervisors to pass out petitions for it on the shop floor.[74] It also failed.

Given such a rocky beginning, why did Boeing's biggest union not develop a more antagonistic relationship with the company? Allen, by most accounts, was not antiworker, and so did not carry a grudge despite the strike or those that followed. And neither, apparently, did the workers. "Like other 'job conscious' unions, Local 751 was interested primarily in better wages and benefits, not a larger role in decision making or access to Boeing's books."[75] Allen, originally from Montana, also had seen the mixed blessing of the often-overbearing Anaconda Mining Company in his home state, and did not think that Boeing should dominate Washington in the same way.[76]

But Allen also was reined in by the government. During contract talks with the Machinists in 1962, he sought an open shop and what McCann describes as various "anti-union" provisions.[77] Still worried about the Cold War, President Kennedy stepped into the negotiations, got a temporary no-strike pledge from the union, and assigned a board to examine the contract offer. The so-called "Boeing Aerospace Board" was extraordinarily critical of the company's offer, which it called punitive.[78] The Washington State senate went so far as to pass a resolution calling on Boeing to offer a fair contract. "Whereas the Boeing Company," it began, "with its thousands of employees in the state of Washington, has a tremendous impact on the economic life of this area, and its work interruption would be a serious occurrence for the entire area,..."[79] The company finally gave in just before the Machinists' strike deadline.

The state senate's verbiage was, in a way, a statement of where the state and the company had gone together, their fates now completely intertwined. It also signaled an impending change in Boeing's relations with the public sector, which up until that point had largely involved the federal

rather than state or local levels of government. Still, it was the federal government's largesse that would make Boeing whole enough to get back into
the commercial aircraft business in a big way. And this would change the
whole equation for Boeing and Washington State.

Ultimately, it was not a quiescent work force that Boeing really needed;
it was contracts. The Cold War and Korea bailed the company out in the
late 1940s and 1950s,[80] before commercial jet airplanes made Boeing a
household word. After the war, Boeing built the first jet bombers, and its
experience with the B-47, the B-52, and the KC-135 tanker helped it build
the 707 on its own in the mid-1950s.[81] While the British Comet was exploding in mid-air (a problem traced to design flaws that resulted in what
designers now call metal fatigue), Boeing was building a jet that changed
the business. (And building for the American market required a product
that had bigger wings and hence more range, a shortcoming of European
jetliners to this day.) Building a commercial jetliner was a gamble, because
airlines were not convinced that they needed to buy new planes. Douglas,
still the number one commercial manufacturer, wavered and consequently
did not have a jet available until 1958.[82] The 707 was solidly in business by
that point.

A legendary incident involving the 707 says a lot about Boeing and its
relation to the Seattle area. In July 1954, with 300,000 Seattleites crowded
around Lake Washington for the annual Seafair hydroplane races, Boeing
test pilot Tex Johnston made a planned fly-by over the lake in the Dash-80,
the prototype of the 707. As Boeing's William Allen and the nation's air
transport executives—in town for a meeting—looked on, Johnston put the
huge new jet through a barrel roll. Then he came back and did it again.
And this was only two months after three Comet disintegrations had
grounded the whole fleet.

It showed, of course, all of Boeing's potential customers that the new
ship could fly. Allen was reportedly furious, although Johnston had prac-
ticed the maneuver and insisted it was not particularly stressful on the airplane. Boeing's public relations director quickly went to work, and no Seattle newspaper published an account, despite the overwhelming number of
spectators. (Mansfield's book does not even mention the event, though
later writers have been braver.)

By 1954, the game had changed. The region and the company had enormous stakes in each other's futures. Boeing had substantial plants and investment in Seattle and Renton; it had a top-drawer engineering school at

the University of Washington; it had the beginnings of generations of workers whose children and grandchildren were going to grow up and work at Boeing. Simply moving away was rapidly becoming an expensive idea in what has never been a high-margin business. It seems evident from the start that the region does not have to do more than meet Boeing's marginal propensity to move. Although by 1952 company officials said they would rather be elsewhere, they ruled it out once they started adding up the cost and time involved.[83]

Boeing officials through the years have developed a stable of basic speeches, the three most common of which are the carrot speech, the stick speech (which Shrontz gave), and the new product speech. The carrot speech actually comes up about as often as the stick speech, but usually is less noticed. Soon after the debut of wings over Wichita (when Boeing was forced by the federal government to move some production east), Allen was moved to comment at a public gathering:

> Furthermore, I recognize that the large employment such as we have in this area—more than 37,500 persons—presents certain community and local problems. We try to do our best to be good citizens in the community. There has been committed in this locality since the first of 1950 $65 million to enable Boeing to do its job. Twenty-five million of that has come out of Boeing funds. That, I believe, is representative enough that we believe in this part of the world and want to stay here and live here and succeed here.[84]

And they did. By 1958, employment was back up to 60,000. "Boeing was so important to metropolitan Seattle that *Business Week* called the place a 'one industry town.'"[85] Homer Bone's 1934 anti-Boeing speech provoked no outcry from the state's newspapers at the time; twenty-five years later Henry Jackson could be "senator from Boeing" and not suffer at all. Jackson, as the more erudite observers have noted, simply recognized the company's importance to his constituents, and so worked with Boeing to help it win contracts, though, it is worth remembering, he did oppose the Allen-supported right-to-work measure of 1958.[86]

Years later, Shrontz acknowledged the company's debt to the region, echoing Allen's speech. But he also raised the specter of the dying rust-belt towns of the Northeast that had been visiting us on the nightly news for much of the 1980s. What was really trenchant about the image Shrontz created was that anybody who had been around Seattle awhile had lived through purgatory and had a good look at hell. After riding its jet transport business and the Apollo program through the 1960s, Boeing nearly crashed and burned as the 1970s arrived. It had grown large and less efficient; the business cycle turned down; and it was betting the company on the 747 and simultaneously building the largest building in the world to put it in. Federal funding for the proposed Super Sonic Transport (SST) was cancelled, and unsold planes began to take up space on the runways. Orders for new planes dried up as the economy contracted; Boeing's order backlog fell by half from 1968 to 1969. Boeing laid off 25,000 workers in 1969, and that was only the beginning, with 41,000 more going out the door in 1970 and 22,000 in 1971.[87] The company booked no new orders in all of 1970. Even the new 747s were grounded, blocks of concrete hung under their wings to maintain the weight to be provided by Pratt & Whitney's unfinished engines. Eugene Rodgers, like a number of observers, concluded that Boeing had tried to do too much, too fast.[88] As Condit said in a speech twenty-five years later: "Boeing came within an eyelash of bankruptcy."

The need to plan ahead and plan carefully was not lost on the young engineers and technocrats who would later run Boeing, including Shrontz, Condit, and Ron Woodard (eventually Commercial Airplane Group president), all of whom survived the bust to see the company recover yet again. Condit said the Boeing Bust "clearly affected the way I think about organizations and the stability of organizations. 'Be more careful when you're going up because on the other side of up is always down.' We went up way too fast. We were not efficient in the process, so when we got to the top, we were way overmanned and the far side was very steep. I do not ever want to do that again."[89] "Darwin was right," Condit told the Association of Washington Cities in 1995. "If you do not respond to conditions, you will go away."

T. Wilson replaced Bill Allen as president in April 1968 and set about to create a leaner, meaner Boeing in short order. Local Boeing employment fell from more than 100,000 in 1967 to under 40,000 in 1971. Seattle-area unemployment soared from 2.5 percent in 1968 to as high as 17 percent in 1971, the worst in the nation. A couple of local real estate salesmen bought a billboard that read, "Will the last person leaving Seattle turn out the lights?"

They were grim times in a town that had not really known them since the Depression. Some people moved, others tried to start new businesses. It moved some to complain that this was all Boeing's fault, that the company had somehow failed the region. Philip Bailey, publisher of a weekly, high-brow newspaper called the *Argus*, sniped, "Boeing really did us in when it brought 50,000 employees into the area to build the 747, which resulted in too much home and apartment building, too much money for schools, too many new taxes and now too much unemployment."[90] Never mind that a lot of those people had been hired locally, or that not building the 747 would have changed Boeing's whole future and with it that of the region, and probably not for the better.

Within ten years, the *Argus* was gone, but Boeing was not. Building the 747 very nearly did bankrupt the company, but Boeing learned from its mistakes, improved its productivity, and carved out a lucrative market niche (jumbo jets) it has had to itself ever since.

The concurrent logic, to be heard with regularity following each subsequent Boeing slump, was that Seattle was not doing enough to diversify its economy. Having participated in a half-dozen economic diversification forums, I believe the options for this are somewhat limited and partially beyond the scope of a city or even a region to employ. But it is a regular and siren call. In Portland, for example, the *Oregonian* newspaper smugly declared, "Now Seattle is paying a terrible price for allowing a single industry to so dominate its economic structure."[91]

David Brewster, former publisher of the *Seattle Weekly*, vaguely the successor of the *Argus*, later argued for a cap on Boeing employment in the area.[92] This assumes some stable level of Boeing employment, which is plainly false. It also underscores one of the great local myths: if Boeing had not been so big, the logic goes, the economy would be more diverse. Well, in one sense it would be, and also smaller. As the economist Dick Conway said in the midst of a recent Boeing downturn, "The economy is diversifying before our eyes." But the myth assumes that something else would have come here in Boeing's place. What? And why? When it is apparent that Boeing was here at all almost completely by chance, that it succeeded because of extraordinary circumstances that had little to do with location and stayed in large part by force of habit, to assume that some other industry would have arisen in its place is the height of foolish hubris. But this myth rolls on like the Columbia River; when Northwest aluminum smelters argued for moderation in electric rates in the 1980s (electricity is by far the single largest cost factor in aluminum production), opponents argued that the plants and their high-paying jobs would not be that big a loss. "We can use the electricity for something else," one advocate told me. No one ever says what "something else" might be, but apparently there is a big catalog of employers out there, and one has only to call up and place an order and new factory jobs arrive by UPS.

Yet the absurdity goes on. Neal R. Peirce, a journalist who specializes in urban affairs and sporadically alights in Seattle for some whirlwind analysis, said the lack of diversity was partially Boeing's fault. "Part of the blame lay with Boeing itself," he said, "which has not encouraged development of many offshoot suppliers within Washington—firms which might then begin to diversify themselves, adding to the economic mix of the area."[93]

Building airplanes, it seems, was not enough. The company was also supposed to take care of everything else. Amid the Boeing Bust of 1969–1971, Peirce further castigated the company for not diversifying its product line, and cast doubt on its prospects: "responsible economists saw nothing on the horizon to suggest a major comeback in the foreseeable future."[94] Responsible for what?

Boeing looked at diversification and concluded it was not as advertised. In the 1960s and '70s, the company made forays into windmills, hydrofoils, rapid transit systems, and turbine engines. Part of the problem facing any aerospace firm moving into more consumer-oriented products is that the tolerances required for things that fly tend to far exceed those required for anything else. "We could build dashboards," said one Seattle-area aerospace executive, whose company made high-tech composites for aircraft. "But it would be more dashboard than you'd ever need."[95]

Boeing sold some rapid transit systems, but found that the vagaries of dealing with municipal governments were not to its liking. It also sold a number of hydrofoils, another fascinating technology that, on the surface, appeared to have enormous potential. Boeing even sold a couple to the state as passenger-only ferries, getting 80 percent of the cost from federal transit funds and then successfully lobbying the state legislature in 1973 and 1977 for the other 20 percent.[96] But it was not a profitable business. "It was not a good environment for shipbuilding," said a naval architect who worked with Boeing, in part because of the different manufacturing requirements imposed on each product line.[97]

The company tried a number of different things, from agriculture to energy and construction management. It pitched the federal government at length about helping the West Coast through the aerospace slump.[98] Boeing sold some windmill systems, but energy prices did not climb the way they were supposed to. The company had leased a large amount of land in

Eastern Oregon in the 1960s, and when its other ideas for it did not fly, attempted to create a large-scale farming operation.[99] Most intriguing were the turbine engines; among other applications, Boeing engineers developed a crackerjack turbine outboard motor. But building the sales and marketing organization needed to distribute the product was more than the company wanted to take on (a decision that rings faintly of American electronics firms' intransigence over the video-cassette recorder in its early days).[100] Some years later, Boeing CEO Phil Condit said the company instead decided to stick to its knitting. "We do not know the market," he said of the things observers often say Boeing ought to be doing. "We do not know the customer."

Throughout Boeing's soaring ups and dismal downs, Seattle carried on. Even when more than 60,000 workers were laid off in the 1969–71 Boeing Bust, fewer than 15 percent of those people relocated out of the region.[101] Some of the new startups survived and prospered. Meanwhile, the wealth of airplanes was ushering in the next economic generation. (Would, for example, William Gates, Sr.'s law firm have grown so large, allowing him to send his son to a private school and to Harvard, from whence he returned to start Microsoft with Paul Allen, if the economy had not grown fat on the region's—and Boeing's—success?)

But Boeing has always spawned two sets of local observers: those who celebrate the company, and those who, as Shrontz put it in his famous speech, "do not think we've done enough." They are similar to the citizens who live here, some of whom like it and some of whom consistently cluck only about its shortcomings. But the local cognoscenti seem to believe that there is a certain cachet to taking on Boeing and so, firing without aiming, they do.

Roger Sale, in his quite enjoyable history of Seattle, argues that Seattle has been not much more than a colony for Boeing. Going a half step further than Peirce, he says that the aerospace giant in some way managed to prevent "spin-off industries" from developing nearby, though he neither says why nor proves his point. One might argue that the problem is Boeing's devotion to a tax structure that is friendly to big firms but hard on start-ups,[102] but Sale does not, and I am not about to do it for him. And, as noted above, hundreds of Boeing sub-contractors operate in Washington State, including the aforementioned firms started by Boeing refugees.[103] More to the point, the presence of Teamsters' boss Dave Beck may have had as much to do with keeping new business out (which Sale points out himself),[104] if not the simple explanation of Seattle's distance from the country's major markets. Pascall, Pedersen, and Conway later concluded that Boeing was in fact the largest supporter of small businesses in the state. Nor did they find that it had hampered the development of other manufacturers.[105] But simple economics never stopped a critic.

Boeing's rise to dominance in commercial aerospace has continually confounded its critics. Douglas Aircraft eventually responded to the 707 with the successful DC-8 and DC-9, but underpriced so many of them that it had to be acquired by McDonnell, whose prior experience was largely as a military contractor.[106] McDonnell did not quite understand the commercial business, according to John Newhouse; unlike the military side of aerospace, one could not just tell the customer, "Here's the product; this is the price."[107] And although later versions of the DC-9 (the MD-80 and -90) sold reasonably well, McDonnell eventually agreed to be acquired by Boeing, its commercial business rapidly becoming a footnote in aviation history.

Other competitors came and went. The Europeans were not successful until they pooled their efforts in the four-nation Airbus Industrie consortium that today is Boeing's chief competitor. Building commercial jets proved to be a disaster for General Dynamics' Consolidated division; Lockheed built the excellent L-1011 but never made money at it because it split that market segment with Douglas' DC-10. Boeing remained alone in the skies with the 400-seat 747, and the big jet made the company a consistent pile of money. It plowed those profits back into improved versions of the 737, the newer 757, and the 767, and then recently launched the giant 777 twinjet, which captured more than 70 percent of its market segment from its introduction in the early 1990s.

Despite Boeing's troubles as a manufacturer—which it has labored long and hard to correct in recent years—it reached the end of the twentieth century as the low-cost producer of commercial jetliners, with a worldwide parts and service network second to none and a reputation for building safe aircraft that, as more than one executive put it, "make money for our customers."

The cyclical nature of the aerospace industry has always driven Boeing on a dessert-or-desert flight path, which has made the company somewhat bulimic as an employer. Airlines routinely order more planes than they can possibly use, because the turnaround times have been so long that they have feared missing out on choice delivery positions. The result for the region was, as the local axiom put it, "When Boeing catches a cold, Seattle catches the flu."

And yet, in the early 1990s, 30,000 Boeing jobs lost through layoffs and attrition—jobs whose wages and productivity dwarfed those of their earlier counterparts'—did not flatten the Seattle economy as did the downturns of 1969 or even 1982. In fact, from 1983 to 1999 the Seattle region suffered no recession at all, even during the national downturn of the early 1990s. In part that was because the company instituted a hiring freeze and its first-ever early retirement offer, thus easing the number of actual layoffs.

But it also was true in part because the economy had diversified. In the 1960s one of every five jobs in King County was at Boeing, but in the 1990s that had shrunk to less than one in ten, a sizable percentage but not the same.[108] Whatever Boeing's economic multiplier, the region simply had too many jobs that did not depend on aerospace. Between Auburn and Tukwila, south of Seattle, is the fifth largest concentration of industrial and warehouse space in the country; the region features the sixth largest high-tech concentration in the nation and the third largest biotech concentration; and together the ports of Seattle and Tacoma comprise one of the largest containerized cargo operations in the world. (Remember Sell's Third Law. As the economy diversified, Boeing's economic and political dominance was destined to wane.)

Throughout the era, the semi-observant continued to predict Seattle's doom. Jane Jacobs, for instance, wrote that the city never developed "a region" (without really saying what that is or how it could be done), and lumped Seattle in with a fistful of rust-belt cities with stagnant economies destined for ruin.[109] And yet in 1994 a visiting bank economist, somewhat more in tune with local events, was moved to say that the old axiom was no longer true: "When Boeing catches a cold, Seattle gets the sniffles."

By 1996, Glenn Pascall himself, reflecting on the earlier study he had co-written, said the change was evident. "You can argue that until some time in the early 1990s, Boeing probably had a larger role in the Washington state economy than any other company," he said. But the company's payroll by then had declined by $700 million even as that of the software industry had risen by $1.2 billion. "Until that shift of economic oomph occurred, not even any one of the Big Three automakers accounted for as large a share of total state employment as Boeing did here."

State treasurer and ex-legislator Dan Grimm agreed. "They are a less significant portion of the economy than they were in the past," he said. And so the rules of the game were changed. The political dominance so long implicit in Boeing's economic dominance began to erode, an erosion to be seen most clearly in the battle over growth.

3 / Flight Path

Growth and Antigrowth

Naturally, people disagree over the kinds of sacrifices that should be
made, and by whom, to produce profits and jobs for others. The goal
of economic growth sometimes seems to conflict with the goal of
preserving or enhancing environmental quality.

—Ken Dolbeare, 1983

I do not know if I want another 200,000 jobs in this region. . . . The
question is, where do we put them?

—Bernie Friedman, Mukilteo City Councilman

I love this region, and it's great for doing business, but it just took us
four and a half months to get a permit to install an air conditioner.

—Stephen Duzan, CEO, Immunex Corporation

IN THE POSTWAR ERA, the issue of growth has arisen with regularity in the
Puget Sound region. World War II spurred phenomenal growth in the
region, and with it a whole new brand of politics:

The relatively high wages paid in this new economy, together with extensive
unionization and the sustained affluence of the wartime years, raised many
people to middle class status. World War II also brought a new wave of middle class immigrants to Washington, many of whom joined Washington residents to build extensive new suburbs around the major cities. These developments combined to blunt the dynamism of the early reform tradition and
to establish a new kind of politics in the state. For the first time Washington
had a socially responsible stratum of people to provide public-interested

33

leadership. Americans generally seemed to accept the newly active role of the federal government, and the same role began to be expected of the state. Washington soon developed a top-down style of politics, in which an acquiescent electorate approved various initiatives and problem-solving actions taken by state government.[1]

The roots of this new conception of government come from the era just before the war. The Great Depression also helped to generate a much more activist form of government in Washington. Dolbeare notes how all the public works projects of the 1930s, particularly roads and bridges, primed the state for later growth.[2] Coupled with federal spending on industry—such as the Defense Plant Corporation's spending on expansion of Boeing plants—the state that emerged from the war years was in many ways different from the state that preceded it.[3]

Growth was not without consequences. Growth-related issues began to sprout as soon as the wartime boom began, including housing shortages, rising crime, fire hazards, public health problems, strains on the transportation system, and overcrowded schools.[4] By 1945, area residents were complaining about untreated sewage fouling local bays,[5] a sure sign of a growing population. The complaints eventually led to the creation of the Municipality of Metropolitan Seattle, a countywide organization that built secondary sewage treatment plants and helped clean up local waters. That task proved easier than dealing with the myriad of growth-related challenges that were to follow.

Given the area's natural advantages (such as mild climate, natural wealth, deep-water harbors), one might have predicted that the Puget Sound region would grow. As the growth took on political and cultural shape, however, the difficulty of dealing with such a broad issue also became evident.

Seattle, with about 500,000 people, is the largest city in Washington State. Its relatively small size (for a metropolis) makes it less a political focal point than other regional centers tend to be.[6] The metropolitan area has about 2.5 million people, however, and King County alone has at least 30 percent of the state's registered voters. Two-thirds of the state's population lives west of the Cascade Mountain range, and one half between Olympia and Bellingham. Physically the smallest of the western states except for Hawaii, it has the smallest percentage of federal land but gets the most federal money and is fourth in federal civilian employment. It is

largely white, with longstanding but small Native, Asian- and African-
American communities.

In the 1970s, L. Harmon Ziegler and Henrik van Dalen wrote that Washington was not economically diverse,[7] which at the close of the twentieth
century appeared to be no longer true, if it ever was. It is true that parts of
the state have been somewhat dependent on a small number of industries,
but overall the state's economy is remarkably varied. One might think of its
core as 4-F: flying, fishing, farming, and forestry. As the twentieth century
drew to a close, software, biotechnology, and trade through Puget Sound
ports became important sectors, while fishing and forestry remained important but have shrunk. Agriculture, in which Washington leads the nation
in production of crops ranging from apples and hops to pea seed and
peaches, still is a large and profitable industry.

The varied economy has produced a political life just as diverse, creating
an odd blend of radical, populist, and mainstream politics, a place where
the growth coalition could thrive, where farmers from the Midwest could
build replicas of the places they left behind, and where mill owners, war
veterans, and the International Workers of the World—the Wobblies—
could shoot and club each other with abandon.

Since the 1940s, it has been a politically competitive state between
Republicans and Democrats, although William F. Mullen and John C. Pierce
characterize it as not a strong party state.[8] Washington is one of the few
places in the country, for example, where voters do not register by party.
In Daniel Elazar's classic typology of political cultures, Washington is cited
as moralistic/individualist, featuring a strong sense of right and wrong, an
activist government, and activist citizens.[9] (In the 1970s, for example, citizens rolled back a legislative salary increase and instituted one the nation's
toughest campaign finance reporting laws.) Ziegler and van Dalen found
that while Washington's political parties were weak, its interest groups were
not, given its assumed lack of economic diversity. Of course, they do not
say how they measure economic diversity, but everybody says the local
economy is not diverse.[10]

Some observers have noted the diversification of the state's economy
and what that means to politics. Elizabeth Walker describes what really is
a plethora of strong interest groups contending in the arena of public
affairs: unions, banks, the forest products industry, business, insurance,
contractors, professional groups, utilities, environmentalists, and Boeing.

"Washington state has experienced economic diversification with a corresponding growth in the number and sophistication of professional lobbyists. Clearly this development facilitates more interest group participation in the political process."[11]

You could easily get the impression that it is all about Boeing, however. You cannot drive around Seattle—especially through South King County or past the south edge of Everett—and not notice what has been called, in good times, the Lazy B. The company has plants in rural Pierce County, Auburn, Kent, Renton, Tukwila, Seattle, Bellevue, and Everett, with office buildings and factories and research facilities scattered across the landscape. It also has a manufacturing facility in Spokane, on the eastern edge of the state, and one in Portland, Oregon, to the south. Boeing's ubiquity leads visitors and newcomers to marvel when they notice it, prompting comments such as Neal Peirce's observation, made in 1972:

> The Boeing Company dominates the economy of a large metropolitan region and a state as no other industrial firm in America. When Boeing is prospering, half of the manufacturing plant workers in the entire Puget Sound area are on its payroll. Then it is that Seattle and the satellite towns glow with economic health, population booms and the future seems forever assured. But when Boeing's orders begin to dwindle seriously, as they did at the start of the 1970s, the result can be widespread unemployment.[12]

Boeing's omnipresence on the economic and physical landscape leads to some understandable assumptions. Asking whether Boeing is politically powerful anywhere near Seattle is likely to produce snickers if not sneers from anyone who has been here awhile. It is just assumed, and not without some reason. Delbert C. Miller, in a 1958 reputational study of Seattle (which he called "Pacific City"), found that the number one "key influential" was a manufacturing executive.[13] In 1958, in Seattle, there was only one manufacturing executive worth mentioning.

"Pacific City" had always been a little uncertain about economic power and growth. At the state constitutional convention in 1888, populists battled railroad and shipping interests. The populists won, getting the "credit clause" inserted into the final document. This prevents virtually every government in the state from lending public money to private interests; the exception for port districts was not added until 1911.[14]

Seattle's economic pioneers once dreamed of making the city "the

Pittsburgh of the West."[15] Locational challenges made such a notion unlikely; Seattle is too far from sources of iron ore, not to mention markets
for steel. Even so, the very idea of becoming a steel town or anything like
one has always produced skepticism among local residents. In fact any
moment of economic stability seems to produce a concern about too much
growth. Cohn spotted the feeling in the early 1950s, when he questioned the
region's apparent dependence on Boeing.

> Ambivalence characterizes the attitude of the people of the Northwest
> toward industrialization. They want more industry: rationally, because they
> realize that more manufacturing will help assure a better-balanced economy,
> and emotionally, because their strong regionalism leads them to desire for
> the Northwest features which other sections of the country enjoy. At the
> same time, however, they point to the crowded, sooty manufacturing cities
> of Pennsylvania and Ohio and protest that they do not want the green valleys
> of the Northwest to look like Pittsburgh. Whereas they say they want more
> industry, they do not mean it wholeheartedly and are reluctant to take steps
> which would encourage its development, such as planning industrial sites,
> improving ports and cargo unloading facilities, and so forth.[16]

It is against this backdrop that the Boeing Company has lived its corporate
life. The company grew, sometimes slowly, sometimes in fits, and the region
grew with it. The company was happy, the region often so. But not always.

Up until at least the 1960s, the state was in a growth mode, doing what
it could in its haphazard way to encourage economic development but
benefiting most from geography, politics, and luck.

> The story of the growth of the state of Washington since 1940 primarily is
> a story of what can be done by defense industries and federal development
> programs. Boeing, the Bremerton Navy Yard, atomic energy development at
> Richland, the Columbia Basin Reclamation Project in central Washington,
> and the new aluminum industry all depend upon federal defense or river
> development projects. Attention to politics, then, has been vital to the econ-
> omy of the state.[17]

Between 1910 and 1940 the state's population remained steadfastly 47 percent rural; by 1950 that number was 37 percent and falling.[18] In the decades
that followed, the Puget Sound region kept growing, and environmental

concerns and quality-of-life issues began to show up in the 1960s and 1970s.[19]

That is about the time growth issues began to show up nationwide, spurred by a growing mistrust of government and corporate America, by relative prosperity, and by a realization of the costs as well as the benefits of growth. General Motors executive Ernest S. Starkman caught the feeling in a net:

> During the decade of the 1960s it would appear that much of America turned sour on itself.... As part of this trend, the American public has become increasingly critical of the profits, prices and policies of the country's largest corporations and, indeed, of the entire economic structure. A recent published poll indicated that two-thirds of the public believes Washington should set ceilings on prices, and one-third thinks the same about profits. Some of the populace would break up larger corporations. And views of intellectual leaders tend to be more critical than those of most others.[20]

The era was witness to a rising number of disputes over siting industrial facilities in "unspoiled natural environments."[21] With the economy booming, the decisions were not always for developers. For example, in the late 1960s, BASF, the German chemical giant, wanted to put a petrochemical plant near Hilton Head, South Carolina. Opposition arose from environmental groups, fishing interests, and the developers of Hilton Head. State government favored the plan, along with other citizens, an antipoverty group, and the NAACP, which understandably did not see much chance for advancement for black Americans in Hilton Head's recreation industry. The plant promised to generate as many as 7,000 jobs. The state sold BASF the land and promised to build a railroad spur and a four-lane highway to the site, to dredge the nearby river, and to give the company five years without any state income tax. But after federal officials stepped in and warned the company about polluting the area's pristine estuary, BASF backed out and built elsewhere. John E. Logan and Arthur B. Moore, Jr., concluded that one of the biggest hurdles was the ineffective and uncertain quality of state and federal environmental laws.[22]

That was already changing. In Washington, at about the same time, state government was finally empowered to act positively with regard to the environment. Economic growth, environmental awareness, and progressive government all came together. "The momentum from this convergence and achievement carried over into the early 1970s, and was expressed with particular strength in the environmental movement."[23] The state legislature passed the State Environmental Policy Act, created a new Department of Ecology (the first state to do so), and voters approved the Shorelines Management Act in 1971.[24] This spirit survived even the chaotic economic times of the 1970s. Some 60,000 citizens participated in a 1975 planning exercise, and their chief concerns were the environment and jobs, in that order. The document called for "moderate" economic growth.[25]

That is not what happened. The state recovered rapidly from the Boeing Bust of 1969–71.[26] Washington's population grew 71 percent in the 1970s, as the Puget Sound region became known as one of the best places to live in the country. All around the Sound, communities logged double- and triple-digit growth as suburbia spread outward from Seattle.[27] Moreover, by the late 1970s, economists and others had concluded that the regional economy had at long last diversified, with more jobs in services, trade, and nonaerospace manufacturing. Boeing's share of manufacturing employment, in fact, had fallen from 36 percent at the beginning of the decade to 21 percent at the end.[28]

And still, as the 1980s approached, many in Washington were unsure of the future. Some clear-headed person might have recognized that the commercial airplane business was highly cyclical, and as long as Boeing was anchored to Seattle, the region should expect to be buffeted by those ups and downs. As it was, for three decades, each of those oscillations was treated as though every turn was a new reality, a permanent fixture on the horizon. But, as KING-TV executive Emory Bundy noted, "There's a tendency to project growth based on present circumstances. Just as it was fashionable in this state to predict long-term declines in the early part of the 1970s, it's natural now to assume a prolonged period of growth."[29]

Bundy was quoted in one of the most interesting local growth studies ever attempted. The Washington State Research Council, a business-backed think tank, greeted the new decade with a fresh report, *Agenda for the Eighties: The Forces Shaping Washington's Future,* of which volume two, *State Growth and the Economy,* is of particular interest. Most of the dozens of business and civic leaders surveyed concluded that the state was in for a long period of sustained growth. Population gains were estimated at 17 to 25 percent, or adding anywhere from 660,000 to 1 million more state residents by 1990. "Washington state can expect all of the problems and virtues that accompany growth during the 1980s," said banker H. Dewayne Kraeger.[30]

Not every prediction was as rosy. A Weyerhaeuser economist, apparently losing sight of what simple supply and demand might do to energy prices, predicted that high oil costs might strangle world trade, while the state's traditional growth industries had largely "matured." "In some respects, the long-term economic outlook is dismal," said Bruce Lippke, manager of marketing and economic research for the timber giant.[31]

But another Weyerhaeuser executive, William Ruckleshaus, was perhaps more perceptive. People were moving to Puget Sound regardless of the economy, he said; they decide to live here, and then they find work.[32]

Bundy, again, predicted what that would mean:

I think a majority of people are in favor of economic growth, but dislike the idea of population growth. Unfortunately, Washington state is not a sovereignty—it cannot limit immigration. And the cost of economic growth is population growth, which could prove to be the most disruptive influence to the lifestyle to which we have grown accustomed.[33]

Taking that a step further, as did a utility executive quoted in the report, at some point diminishing marginal returns would set in, discouraging further immigration—by all accounts the chief source of the state's rapid growth.[34] Perhaps without realizing it, a local bank economist largely predicted what was going to happen:

Migration could be discouraged by curtailing growth in the economy through creating a state tax and regulatory climate inimical to business expansion. But I doubt this would be acceptable to present residents. An appropriate state posture should involve planning in order to accommodate growth with a minimum negative environmental and social impact.[35]

Meanwhile, at the dawn of the decade, Boeing's prospects once again looked good. It had 60 percent of the commercial jetliner market, shiny new models in the 757 and 767, and it was winning its share of defense contracts. Boeing economist Vincent Helman said the company had worked to try to flatten out its boom and bust cycle by parting out more work to outside suppliers.[36]

Outside forces intervened amid the rosy glow of the Reagan era. Federal Reserve Chairman Paul Volcker's experiment with strict monetarism helped produce the deepest recession since before World War II. The local economy was hammered across the board, and the timber and aerospace industries both got clobbered.

Thus the growth question did not arise in the public consciousness until late in the decade. The recovery that followed, beginning in 1983, was a welcome relief from high unemployment, and the recession appeared to have bled inflation out of the economy. Up until the mid-1980s, what Seattle people remembered and talked about in the Puget Sound region were the fearful days of Boeing layoffs—after World War II, in 1969–70, and in 1982 (when the author was laid off from a newspaper job as the economy rapidly withered).

In 1984, for example, House Democratic Policy Committee economist Rich Nafziger could write, with some justification, that whatever the talk of recovery, the economy was not doing all that well. State unemployment still lingered at 11 percent.[37] But his analysis may help explain why, in only a few years, state policymakers would have such a hard time grasping what growth management might mean for the economy.

> One long-time problem in Washington is the instability of the aerospace industry. Frequent layoffs caused by federal policies have had devastating effects on the state of Washington. Currently, Boeing's business is driven by federal government priorities. Unfortunately, many of those federal policies have not been in Washington's best interests. Not only have they made employment in the Washington [sic] unstable, but Boeing's nuclear missiles [sic] production contributes to the instability of the entire world. We need to develop a system of tax incentives and penalties which will push Boeing towards diversifying away from military programs towards more stable production.[38]

Nafziger follows a thread of analysis that is common to casual Boeing watchers, especially those tending toward the left, driven more by opposition to military spending than by facts. An uneven, leftist, and very interesting analysis done in 1974 by something calling itself the Pacific Northwest Research Center, even while noting that half the commercial jets in the sky came from Boeing, said the company's commercial business just did not matter. "But, as Boeing admits [where? when?]," the unnamed authors wrote, "the appearance that they were largely a part of the civilian economy is illusory.... The Boeing Company is one of a number of industrial giants who will stay permanently on the military dole, producing extravagent [sic] and costly weapons for America's next Vietnam."[39]

Nafziger and Dolbeare (1988) each explain both the 1969–71 and 1981–82 downturns as defense-driven.[40] Actually, both had everything to do with the order cycle for commercial aircraft and very little to do with military spending. At the start of 1968, Boeing had a backlog of orders for 328 commercial aircraft, worth about $2.6 billion at the time. By 1969 the backlog had fallen to 164 jets, and no new orders had been booked for months.[41] The genesis of the blame-the-military analysis seems to be the fact that when the cyclical jetliner market is down, Boeing derives a relatively higher share of its profit from military sales than from commercial sales. However, in most years, commercial sales comprise the bulk of Boeing's sales and profits. And even in 1971, at the depth of the Boeing bust, the company employed roughly twice as many workers in commercial operations as in defense and space work.[42] In the 1980s and 1990s the company generated up to 80 percent of its sales and sometimes all of its profit from commercial work.

Nafziger lauded Boeing's efforts at producing transit systems and wind turbines,[43] but failed to notice that the company did not make any money on those projects. And even as he noted that military contracts comprised only 32 percent of Boeing's business, or about as high as it had been in the commercial jet era, he failed to recognize that orders for civilian jetliners were what really drove Boeing's ups and downs.

> Employment in aerospace is unstable. During times when military spending and space programs are popular, the industry booms. When government policy changes, thousands of people are laid off.... In 1971, when government space and military programs were cut back, employment in Washington aerospace fell from 105,000 to 40,000 in a period of two years....[44]

Most of the cutting was done by 1971, and it had precious little to do with anything other than orders for jetliners and the cost of developing the 747. If one of the leading advisers of state house Democrats understood the company no better—using research that sloppy—one cannot be surprised that the caucus would later rush blindly into growth management.

But, for the most part, growth was not widely anticipated. Demographers expected slow growth through at least 2010.[45] Fostering growth remained the issue. In 1985, the legislature created the Washington State Economic Development Board, "to create a long-term economic development strategy for the state."[46] The board, in its initial report, called for "a more balanced tax system,"[47] an annual quality of life report, and a state mediation service for "resolution of natural resource and development disputes."[48] The report declared that economic growth enhances quality of life, while admitting that traffic congestion, pollution, and loss of open space can detract from quality of life.[49] Typically, the idea that growth might cause those things was not mentioned. In volume two of the report, even the extraordinarily erudite Dick Conway wrote, "Quality of life is seen as an economic asset that must be managed, preserved and marketed."[50] The marketing that the national media did for the region was soon nearly to prove its undoing.

The economy recovered, nationally and locally, and by the late 1980s, the memory of the last recession, little more than half a decade old, was dim and stale. At the end of the decade, the predictions of 1980 began to ring true. Rather suddenly, what people talked about and worried about most was growth—not too little, but too much. Seattle had established an apparently dedicated spot among the lists of the nation's most livable cities. Boeing employment was on its way toward an all-time high of 104,000 in the Puget Sound region. And the company was making plans for expansion.

In 1988 a study by the regional Puget Sound Council of Governments predicted that the population of King, Pierce, Snohomish, and Kitsap counties (the accepted boundaries of the Central Puget Sound region) would soon grow by 600,000 to 3.1 million people, with half the growth coming in King County.[51] Local media, with typical shortsightedness, seized on the topic as cause du jour: "The face of change is unpleasant," declared one reporter, in print. "A lifestyle that was the envy of the nation seems at risk."[52] Never mind that the cyclicality of the local economy, the economics of diminishing marginal returns, and the simple constraints of space made such growth projections at least questionable, the prospect of rampant growth again raised the specter of everything that Northwesterners think is wrong with California. "They're turning it into another Orange County," complained a prominent architect.[53]

Seattle Post-Intelligencer columnist Mike Layton seemed to understand what that meant: "One of these years, some political candidate is going to make a campaign issue of promoting growth and score big at the polls, and suddenly everybody's going to be surprised."[54] Growth advocates, he said, were nineteenth-century thinkers. Whatever the reality of Puget Sound being overwhelmed by growth, people did worry about it. Surveys showed genuine and widespread concern about what growth would do to the town that no longer called itself the Jet City or the Queen City, but the Emerald City.[55] The most-mentioned problem was traffic congestion, in which Seattle ranked as highly nationwide as it did for livability.[56]

In some senses, Boeing had only itself to thank for the growth. All of its success had created a region that would attract and could support more people. Seattle would probably have been a smaller city without Boeing. But even as the economy gloried in full bloom, the Paradox of Growth began to uncoil, slither out of the bushes, and bite. The region's growth, fostered in no small part by Boeing's continued success, drove the community to try to deal with growth's externalities.

The battle lines were being sketched. The *Seattle Times* opened up its wallet in 1989 and brought back Neal Peirce, who stayed ten days and pronounced that the region should stop sprawl by stopping "new building, sewer and water permits in most unincorporated areas."[57] Peirce favored an idea dear to a number of civic planners, "urban villages" that would channel growth into already developed areas.[58] The *Times* also dragooned a panel of business leaders to review Peirce's seven-part series. Presaging the coming debate over the problems and possibilities of growth management, the panel questioned what limits on growth would do to housing prices and costs, and whether it would protect anybody from anything.[59]

The region's response to the new spurt of growth spoke directly to the Paradox: having gathered up growth's benefits, governments and citizens tried to deal with its costs. Seattle citizens overwhelmingly passed a limit on the height of downtown construction, against the wishes of what anyone would easily identify as the growth coalition. "Seattle thus becomes the latest city to leap aboard the slow-growth caravan that has moved up and down the west coast since San Francisco imposed controls on construction in 1985," said *The Economist*, and the city council enacted interim controls even before the election.[60]

Meanwhile, "sensible growth" candidates won victories in local elections. And councils, commissions, and panels that once had been studying economic diversification now turned their eyes toward growth management. But the area lacked a regional government with teeth enough to make any solution stick, and citizens generally opposed items such as tax reform or mass transit that might speak to growth management. "Our present system of local governance ... is today a major impediment to rational and timely public decision making," concluded one study in 1987. "Our ability to plan and execute efficiently is seriously impaired."[61] Corr said that the city and region had risen up and confronted growth in the late 1960s.[62] A nice thought, but typically wide of the mark. Although environmental laws were passed, citizens defeated a measure to fund mass transit, ensuring that the road network would be forever clogged. Missing in this analysis—and in most of the hand wringing that paralleled it—was that at the peak of the late 1960s growth spurt, Boeing employment plummeted. And with it went growth.

Wes Uhlman, who was mayor of Seattle at the time of the 1969–71 Boeing Bust, thought the experience had tempered both the company's approach to the region and the region's approach to the company. "They need the community as well as we need them," he said. "We had to lay off cops and firemen and all kinds of things that cities shouldn't be doing, but we had to do it because we did not have the money. That is when I came to an absolute full appreciation of Boeing." That began to change, however, as the memory of hard times receded like an outbound jet. "The prosperity of the 1980s really blinded some local politicians to the value of Boeing," Uhlman said.

Boeing was not predicting any more downturns anything like its last two, however. The company had made a careful effort to build a backlog of orders so enormous (over $100 billion worth of jetliners at one point) that its business and employment level would be shielded from the eventual cyclic drop in demand for aircraft.[63] The company added 43,000 jobs to its Puget Sound–area payroll between 1983 and 1989,[64] at a time when the rest of the economy was surging ahead. Growth, it seemed, was here to stay. "In a time when the state's economy is booming and no severe crisis is at hand, the specter of California-style sprawl swallowing up the state has captured public attention," one journalist observed.[65]

It certainly had. Despite some business opposition, on April 1, 1990, the Washington State legislature pushed through the Growth Management Act (the GMA), delayed only by necessary compromise between the Democrat-controlled house and the Republican-controlled senate. Despite the date, they weren't kidding. The act required local governments to do a number of things, including the siting of important public facilities, making plans for channeling growth to specified areas, and designating some areas as either growth or nongrowth corridors. It required that services such as schools, water, sewer, and roads be in place before large-scale developments took place. The twelve most populous counties in the state had to write comprehensive land-use plans. In its preamble, the measure stated:

> The legislature finds that uncoordinated and unplanned growth, together with a lack of common goals expressing the public's interest in the conservation and the wise use of our lands, pose a threat to the environment, sustainable economic development, and the health, safety, and high quality of life enjoyed by residents of this state. It is in the public interest that citizens, communities, local governments, and the private sector cooperate and coordinate with one another in comprehensive land use planning. Further, the legislature finds that it is in the public interest that economic development programs be shared with communities experiencing insufficient economic growth.[66]

Some economic development was on the way. Boeing announced on October 15, 1990, that it was going to build an all-new jetliner, the 777. It was to be the first all-digital airplane, built hand in hand with customers, with mechanics and engineers breaking down barriers to solve problems ahead of time that typically plagued new aircraft. Although some critics sniffed (and still do) that Boeing was too late in introducing what became the world's largest twinjet, early sales were brisk, and it looked, on paper, like a better aircraft than the MD-11s and A330/340s it would be competing with. However, building it would require what amounted to a new building, pasted onto the side of the Everett plant, already the world's largest structure by volume. Part of the space would come from a facility to be built on 527 acres purchased in Frederickson in eastern Pierce County, but most of the change would be in Everett. Boeing was certainly aware of what this kind of growth meant to the region. Shrontz said the choice of Frederickson was made in part because siting a plant outside the urban core posed fewer environmental challenges.[67]

The antigrowth coalition was not satisfied with the legislature's work, however, and got a growth management measure on the November 1990 ballot. Considered Draconian in many circles, Initiative 547 failed by a two-to-one margin at the polls, but apparently did well enough to set the stage for some kind of public action. Environmentalists threatened another, improved antigrowth initiative if the legislature did not act. Majority Democrats in the legislature were expected to respond affirmatively, making revisions to give the GMA some canines.[68] In the consensual politics of Washington State, it appeared the state had reached a consensus on growth.

The GMA, meanwhile, had created a Growth Strategies Commission (the usual collection of business, labor, and government leaders) to help sort things out. The commission included the former Boeing chairman T. A. Wilson, who was still on Boeing's board of directors and who surely would have raised hell had he seen anything amiss. Its chairman was Richard Ford, the prominent attorney who only months before had criticized Peirce's growth management suggestions (which in the end were not so far from what was in the GMA). The commission recommended a number of steps in growth management, including urban growth boundaries and provisions for affordable housing. That limiting the supply of land for housing would inevitably raise the price of housing apparently was not considered.[69]

The Growth Management Act's passage was noted without excessive fanfare or controversy. In fact, the largest business lobby endorsed the bulk of the legislation, except for some developers who opposed it.[70] Aside from those with a sharp interest in the issue, public understanding of it was probably low. In a 1993 survey of Seattle-area business owners, 44 percent said they had little or no understanding of the act, and 27 percent said they understood it "somewhat."[71] It eventually had a particular impact on Boeing, and a widespread impact on the state.

It was a typical, predictable, and somewhat haphazard response to economic change in the state. In 1983, in a little-noticed monograph produced by researchers at The Evergreen State College—the state's alternative institution, scorned by many for its radical approach to most of life—the eminent political scientist Ken Dolbeare described the difficulty of what state legislators were trying to do. "There has been little or no overall planning or coordination of state public policies with respect to the economic development of the state," he said, writing at a time when the state and nation were just pulling out of the worst recession since the 1930s.[72] But more presciently, perhaps, he described just how difficult a task growth management was going to be:

> Perhaps the most difficult task is that of harmonizing state policies in such fields as regulation, taxation and expenditure with programs and goals in economic development. In principle it is obvious that economic development is not a separable component. All the subjects acted upon by economic

development policies are also affected simultaneously by revenue and spending patterns and a large number of state and local regulations. But, in practice, each of the other areas has its own history, public constituency, legislative oversight, administrative agency, and program goals. It can be very
difficult indeed to avoid conflict between such established commitments and
the programs and goals of economic development. Mutual cancellation of
efforts is often the result.[73]

Growth was neither inevitable nor endless. The GMA passed the legislature on April 1, 1990, although by March the rate of growth in state
personal income had started falling and Boeing was no longer hiring.
Governor Booth Gardner had planted the seeds of growth management,
however, and was determined to harvest them. In December he unveiled
new legislation designed to strengthen the GMA, requiring more specific
guidelines for local land-use plans, more protection for environmentally
sensitive lands, and a statewide open-space plan.[74] The struggle over the
amendments was somewhat tougher, however, and it took a twenty-day
special session in June 1991 to finally push the legislation through. Boeing
apparently opposed what became the final version of the bill, but could not
derail it. The revisions gave the state the power to force cities and counties
to comply with the GMA, promising loss of state revenues as a penalty.
It provided for more sensitive-areas protection and coordination of planning between governments. It also created three regional boards to settle
disputes, which appeared to be quite similar to the growth management
boards that Gardner and others had opposed in Initiative 547. Environmentalists and legislative leaders seemed to favor the bill, and even a leading business lobbyist pronounced it livable.[75] "This bill ... provides a proper
balance between the interests of business, local government, and the environmental community, and will serve as a practical framework for growth
management in the coming years," Gardner said when he signed the legislation into law.[76]

Growth, however, was soon to take a back seat to other issues. In late
1991 Boeing announced that orders were losing altitude and that it was
instituting a hiring freeze. Within months the company was speaking
openly of layoffs, its countercyclical strategy overwhelmed by the steepest
downturn in the history of the aerospace business. Its airline customers,
hammered by worldwide recession and customers' fear of flying due to the

Persian Gulf War, were in the process of losing what would eventually add up to $12 billion, or more money than they had made in the entire history of the industry. Weakened carriers, desperate for market share, engaged in suicidal fare wars that drove prices so low that operators were losing money on many flights (one analyst called them "a cordless bungie jump"). Airlines not only stopped placing orders for jets, they were deferring and even canceling the orders they had already made. Some observers blamed deregulation, while others pointed to bad business practices. ("They should be taken out and shot," one industry figure said of airline executives.) Either way, orders for new jets fell off the table and Boeing stopped growing and started shrinking.

From a peak of 104,000 in 1990, Boeing's payroll steadily dropped. The company announced it would cut 10,000 jobs in 1993, and almost as many in the following two years, as it slashed output of most of its commercial jetliners. Seattle-area job growth, frequently cited by Conway and others as the most reliable measure of the local economy, crumbled with it (though it never went negative, and the area did not actually suffer a measurable recession). Panels and civic leaders who had spent their time on growth management shifted gears yet again and began to pursue economic diversification and development as the new policy grail. Boeing's cuts, by some estimates, would punch a $320-million hole in the state budget, spurring cuts in state and local public employment.[77] (Realtors and builders feared that the GMA would create a housing shortfall.[78] But Boeing's downturn served to moderate demand and hence housing prices, at least temporarily grounding any notion of a shortage.)[79]

In the midst of this, Shrontz made his speech. It was not the news anyone wanted to hear; Boeing was the thing that always was, the bulwark, the foundation. It sent shock waves through public policy circles, at least, and seemed less-welcome news even than reports of impending layoffs. Unimaginable to everyone was that little more than a year later Shrontz would be on the cover of *Fortune* magazine in an article trumpeting Seattle as the best city in the country for business. In the article, Shrontz said the company could have built a 777 plant for a lot less money in Wichita, but acknowledged that he probably could not have persuaded many of his workers to move there.[80]

Some years later, the economist and former state revenue director Glenn Pascall said he thought Shrontz's speech was a gamble. "I think he took a real risk in saying that, and I think the risk paid off. In a state like ours that really prizes political discourse, that kind of shot across the bow could have backfired. I think it played remarkably well, and it put some serious talk into regulatory reform." The speech was not without supporting evidence, either: in 1986, Boeing had in fact gone to Texas to build a 200-employee defense electronics plant. At the time, Shrontz personally notified Governor Gardner of the move, and assured him that it did not reflect on how Boeing felt about the state.[81]

But business climate rather rapidly if quietly became the company's new cause, as Shrontz's complaints were discreetly echoed by Boeing executives with regularity over the next few years. Boeing officials' comments emphasized what the company saw as the global pressures of competition. But they also revealed just how difficult the Paradox was (and is), inasmuch as Boeing ultimately wanted some of the very items the GMA hoped to ensure. In testimony before the Metropolitan King County Council, Boeing senior vice-president Douglas Beighle said,

> Boeing is in an extremely competitive business worldwide and we are undergoing massive changes to stay ahead.... We have sent almost all our management to World Class Competitiveness training, and we will be sending all of our employees to that training. We are targeting substantial cost reductions in our products, eliminating non-value-added activities and substantially reducing product cycle time. We will have difficulty in remaining world class if the locales where our employees live and work do not provide world class infrastructure such as schools, transportation and other responsibilities of municipal government.[82]

Beighle also called on government to follow Boeing's lead and reinvent itself to improve its processes. For it was the cost and time of getting building permits in Renton and Everett—costs and times driven in large part by the cities' response to growth and growth management—that were moving Boeing to complain.

> We have marvelous resources at Boeing that allow us to design, build and sell world class airplanes, but even with all of these resources we find ourselves stymied when it comes to building facilities. We cannot get through the regulatory and statutory thicket in order to obtain the necessary facilities. The problem is getting worse and not better.[83]

Boeing executives' presentations did not neglect Boeing's particular complaints, but always attempted to the paint the scenario as one that had much broader implications. For example, following Beighle at the County Council, Boeing facilities vice-president Andy Gay spelled it out: "Where this regulatory environment hits hardest is the small business which does not have the option of moving its work to Huntsville, Wichita, Dallas or elsewhere. Regulatory modernization will have a greater benefit in King County on businesses other than Boeing."[84]

Boeing trumpeted that theme across the state. Phil Condit, then president of Boeing, told the Association of Washington Business's annual political gathering that regulatory concerns affect small businesses as well as large ones. "Literally thousands of decisions are made every week about whether I will grow here or somewhere else," he said in 1995. "This isn't a Boeing problem, this is a business problem generally. If this was just a Boeing problem I wouldn't be standing here talking about it." It was the kind of consensual politics typical of Washington State, and equally typical of Boeing's approach to public policy: find allies; build a coalition; attack on all fronts.

4 / Full Court Press

Boeing Confronts the Paradox

The company is also influential in other ways, contributing millions to education and charity, and dominating state politics. It is almost as hard to think of Seattle without Boeing as it is to think of Detroit without General Motors.

—*The Economist*, January 30, 1993

We're working hard to become the employer of choice.

—Ron Woodard, president, Boeing Commercial Airplane Group

IF BOEING WANTED political change, it appeared to have put itself in the best possible position to get it. The company typically neglected little in its approach to Puget Sound. Strategically, entwining itself into the fiber of the community proceeded from two goals: first, and the reason most mentioned by the company, to ensure enhanced quality of life for its employees, which also eases recruiting efforts; second, to enhance the company's image and make it easier to advance policy initiatives. Company executives often speak of feeling some obligation to be a good corporate citizen, and I am not so cynical as to conclude that no altruism is involved. It's their quality of life, too. The last three chairmen (Wilson, Shrontz, and Condit) have lived in upscale parts of town, but not in the gated, exclusive splendor of the Highlands, as did Bill Boeing and William Allen. (Though Condit did ultimately build himself a not-so-humble cottage in the Cascade foothills.)

Boeing's efforts to keep the region happy are broad and deep. Shrontz took on the improvement of K-12 education as a personal crusade, dragooning Boeing staff to get involved in myriad but relatively low-key efforts. Notably, those efforts did not include support for initiatives on private school vouchers or charter schools.

As well as being the largest employer, Boeing also is the region's largest supporter of charities. Chris Jones, the manager in charge of charitable contributions (aside from those for schools), said the company turns down a hundred requests a month from all over the world. Of the $60 million Boeing and its employees give annually, money goes to education (40 to 45 percent), health and human services, cultural organizations, and civic efforts. Donations include both cash and services such as printing and technical support; in 1994, the company gave $27 million in cash and $8.3 million in kind. In fat years, the company pays into a trust so that it is not forced to cut contributions in lean years. In-kind contributions, for example, have included loaning the company's in-house moving operation to projects such as relocating the Washington Talking Book and Braille Library. "The public relations value for Boeing was immense—and with portions of the community that would normally have little to do with Boeing," said one volunteer.

Education funds go to everything from minority scholarships to summer internships, support for minority and independent colleges, and capital campaigns for new facilities. Social service money has gone to shelters for abused and recovering children and to youth services. Shrontz was Seattle-area United Way chairman in 1995. He repeated a familiar Boeing theme in a United Way pitch to a group of South King County Rotarians: "It's clear we must keep this community strong for both our self-interest and because clearly it's the right thing to do." Shrontz later explained part of Boeing's self-interest, a view that underscored the company's oft-spoken concern about "quality of life": "We think it's important in terms of attracting and keeping the kind of people we want." The degree to which he took the task seriously was evidenced by his appointment of the recently retired Bud Coffey (for thirty years, Boeing's chief lobbyist, and widely regarded as the most influential unelected person in the state) as point man in drumming up corporate donations for United Way.

Boeing's support for the arts is evident on every theater, dance, and music program in the region, where it is invariably listed among the top financial donors. Boeing executives frequently are found on boards of directors of such organizations, and Boeing managers are loaned out for fundraising and construction projects. Boeing provides major funding for the Museum of Flight in Seattle, where a number of historic Boeing aircraft are prominently displayed. Civic efforts have ranged from affordable housing projects to a symphony hall to economic development. "Everything we do is focused where our facilities are, where our employees work and live," Jones said.

Nonetheless, other corporate executives sometimes express frustration that the company does not get more widespread community recognition for its efforts, and any big donation from Bill Gates is likely to get more ink and airtime than are Boeing's comparatively larger contributions. But it is to Boeing that community leaders often turn when they need help on one issue or another. "Boeing is the first to be tapped when there's a major crusade under way," said Glenn Pascall, the economist and former state revenue director. But Boeing moves alone on few if any issues, he said. "Boeing has developed its own guidelines: 'We'll be there in proportion to the other players. Do not come to us for the whole $100,000.'" Thus it was that Shrontz became a minority owner of the Seattle Mariners when U.S. Senator Slade Gorton assembled a group to keep them in town; and Boeing superlobbyist Coffey was hauled out of retirement to help assemble financing packages for new baseball and football stadia.

These things did not go completely unnoticed, and Shrontz's tenure as chairman did seem to bring more attention to the company's image. Executives talked more about what the company was doing in the community, and the company began to produce regular reports about its charitable activities.

More important, perhaps, from a business perspective, Boeing moved to shore up its image on Wall Street in the 1990s. With a historically cyclical line of work, the stock occasionally takes a beating (although from the early 1970s to the early 1990s, Boeing was the biggest gainer among the Dow Jones Industrials. A $10,000 investment in Boeing 1973 was worth more than $1 million in 1993). One significant move appears to have been hiring Larry Bishop, who began to work the Street selling the company's story, particularly to institutional investors but also to brokerage houses. Concurrently, Boeing executives began stressing "shareholder value" as one of their essential criteria for success.

Bishop would never claim credit for what happened, however. "What I try to do is communicate to this specialized audience," Bishop said in 1995. Low-key, well-dressed, even-spoken, he seemed ideally suited to the task, and as Boeing's stock spent most of 1996 in the $90-a-share range (up from $30 to $40 two years earlier, breaking into the low 100s in 1997), his efforts appeared to have been successful. "It's fun to tell the story," Bishop said. "It's a fun company to talk about. I'm not sure even some of our management people realize Boeing is such a big deal." Bishop would demur if asked whether he helped the stock's remarkable run-up, but in late 1996 he was promoted to vice-president for communications. No one at Boeing would have been rewarded like that if he or she had failed.[1]

This part of the full-court press includes tactics used by many large firms, such as bringing analysts out for visits and sending top executives to meet with large shareholders. Over a number of years, even skeptical analysts seemed to come around. (One of my personal favorites used to start many of our conversations by saying "Boeing is so full of shit," but in the end, even he had converted to a solid "buy" rating on the stock.)

Boeing's success on Wall Street likely echoed down Main Street as well. On the home front, it would tend to further undergird the company's reputation and perceived civic value; if nothing else, many thousands of Puget Sound residents who do not work for Boeing have purchased shares of the company. (Boeing officials say they do not have any estimate of the number, but many local brokers comment on Northwest investors' penchant for buying local stocks, including Boeing's.)

Boeing further cements its place in the rain by encouraging employees to run for public office or otherwise be involved. "We spend a lot of time helping governments," said Bud Coffey, then Boeing vice-president for governmental affairs, from loaning executives to various civic endeavors to "tons of people elected" to public office. "We encourage people to be involved," he said. "Most of our people are darned good public servants."

In the 1960s, the company went so far as to offer civic involvement training for Boeing employees, and William Allen, then chairman, largely expected that Boeing employees in public office were there to do Boeing's business. That changed under Allen's successor, however. T. Wilson brought on Coffey and a more subtle approach to public policy. "I remember Bill Allen telling me that he'd never voted Democrat in his life, and never expected to," said Gary Grant, a former Democrat state senator and Boeing employee. "I do not think he liked politicians." "When Allen went out and T. Wilson came in, they started treating you like people," said A. N. "Bud" Shinpoch, who spent thirty years at Boeing and almost that long in the legislature and state government. The company acknowledged that "you had a job to do and a responsibility and it wasn't necessarily to support Boeing."

Jim Horn was one of the legion of freshly scrubbed young men who earned engineering degrees in the 1950s and 1960s, and stayed in or came to Seattle to join the burgeoning field of aerospace. Horn's Boeing career

started in 1962 and took him through various states of program management, including work on the Apollo program and the SST. He moved to
the exclusive community of Mercer Island in 1968, and spent sixteen years
on the city council there. After twenty-six years at Boeing, in 1988 he ran
for the state legislature and won. "Boeing encourages people to become
active in the political world," Horn said, and his legislative campaign was
supported by Coffey and by Horn's boss, Defense and Space Group president Jerry King.

Horn said being elected results in a contractual agreement with Boeing.
"You target a given number of days when you think you're going to be
gone," he said. "Boeing tries to make sure you stay on the payroll. You do
not suffer a setback for running for legislator. Upper management recognizes the benefit you may have for being a legislator." But Horn and other
Boeing politicians acknowledge that a big trade-off was involved. Being
away from the job meant being away from the job; the manager or engineer
who serves in a government post may be valuable to the company politically, but in terms of building airplanes and spacecraft, he or she is an
also-ran.

Being gone "is a load on your immediate boss," Horn said. "When
there's a tough job to get done and you're not there, you're not the one."
Promotions and merit raises, which are based in part on assessments from
managers above you, will come more slowly, if at all. "Peers pass you by,"
Horn said. "It's like if you're going to school and you get held back a grade."
"It can't help your career," said Shinpoch. "When I was at work, I probably
spent a third of my time on legislative stuff. It is not that Boeing puts you
in a deep freeze, but if you're not there to do things [all the time] there's
a limited number of things for you to do."

Horn had no complaints, however. "I think Boeing is very good about
this situation," he said. "It would probably be more difficult in a smaller
company." The company did not pressure him on specific issues, Horn
said. "Boeing never lobbied me while I've been in the legislature," Horn
said. "They told me there would be a hands-off situation." Another of the
relative handful of recent Boeing legislators, the late Bruce Holland, spent
most of his time working on education and budget issues; the fact that he
worked for Boeing largely went unnoticed.

Horn acknowledged that he did get campaign contributions from the
company, and Boeing lobbyists attended his fund-raisers. "I see more of
them now that I've retired (from Boeing)," he said. Horn said that in six

years in the legislature he did not vote against Boeing, but then he did not vote against business much anyway. For example, Horn sported a 100 percent rating from the National Federation of Independent Businesses, a small-business lobby. By 1994, however, Boeing had no active employees in the legislature. "That disturbs me," said Coffey.

In recent decades, Boeing also avoided political confrontation with what had been a countervailing force for other large firms: its labor unions. In Michigan, for example, the legislature was a regular battleground between the automakers and the United Auto Workers.[2] As noted above, at least since the end of William Allen's tenure as CEO, Boeing has enjoyed amiable relations with its unions despite frequently tough negotiations and at least one strike per decade.

The parochialism that the region is so often chided for may also play a role. Boeing employees typically want to live in the Seattle area, and they do not mind working for Boeing. Rodgers notes, for example, that the company averages only about fifty grievances a year, versus 3,000 to 4,000 for a typical firm of this size, and employees seemed to quickly forgive the company for a bitter, sixty-nine-day strike in 1995.[3] Longtime union official Bill Walkama said as much:

> The relationship between the union and the Boeing Company has probably never been better. There's an ongoing meeting process. . . . The whole thinking has changed. Today, the company seeks our cooperation. I think they really want to be competitive. They know that if they're going to be competitive, they have to work with us to make it happen. . . . When Allen left, things got better.[4]

In recent years, Machinists' membership has swung between 24,000 and 50,000 workers, depending on where Boeing is in its order/production cycle. The Machinists have gone on strike at least once every dozen years, most recently in 1995, and battled the company over a number of work-related issues, including what they see as trading jobs for plane sales. But, fundamentally, the Machinists, like most Boeing workers, are very well paid (they average $40,000 a year), with a remarkable degree of pride in their product. The unveiling of the new 777 (choreographed by Dick Clark Productions) drew close to 100,000 employees and their families in 1995. Enough dewy-eyed engineers and mechanics were in attendance to suggest that it meant something to them. In 1992 Tom Baker, then president of

District Lodge 751, said, "We'd go to the wall for this company if we thought they were really in trouble," and he appeared to mean it.

Job security is one of the biggest sources of friction between Boeing and the Machinists. The Machinists and others have charged Boeing with off-loading jobs to firms in foreign markets in order to sell aircraft. Officially, such off-set agreements are barred by the rules of world trade, and if you believe that, go home, get the checkbook, and buy a clue. Nonetheless, if the alternative is not selling those aircraft, then nobody has a job, and it is hard to see how that is better. Boeing probably is a bit shortsighted when it comes to how it values its workers, and certainly there are times when the company ought to think twice about the real cost of shipping work to sub-contractors when it does not have to. But by 1996 the company had offered to retrain anybody for a comparable job affected by off-loading. Boeing also adopted a tax-free stock incentive plan for all employees, essentially letting everybody share in gains in the price of stock.

It is also easy to argue, as some have, that Boeing's layoffs in the first half of the 1990s were simply too deep. At the time, the company argued that it had to trim employment to cope with the sharp downturn in aircraft orders, "or there won't be any jobs left for any of us," as Boeing managers often put it. Ironically, the company remained profitable throughout the downturn. When it had to hire thousands of new employees to ramp up production when the order cycle turned in 1996, things went so awry that Boeing eventually took more than $3 billion in write-offs to cover the cost of fixing its own mistakes. Surely, $3 billion would have kept layoffs to a minimum with cash left over. Conversely, however, no one—from Boeing and Airbus officials to the most optimistic stock analysts—expected the jet market to recover as quickly and rapidly as it did. In any event, neither off-loading nor layoffs appear to have had much impact on local politics, except perhaps to rally employees around Boeing's flag in its efforts to control locally imposed costs.

Its second largest union, the 20,000-member Society for Professional Engineering Employees in Aerospace (perhaps the largest white-collar union in the world), spends a lot of its time trying to persuade the company that it can do things better. SPEEA staged a one-day walkout in 1993, and a forty-day strike in 1999. It bargains over a host of economic questions, but also enjoys relatively high salaries and decent working conditions.

As a consequence, the company and its unions do not spend a lot of time at each other's throats. Frequently, when faced with competitive challenges, the unions back the company. In 1991, as the company sought approval for its Everett plant expansion, dozens of Machinists barraged Snohomish County Council members to discourage an appeal of expansion of the Everett site. They were urged on by Baker.[5]

"There are times when we can work together," said Linda Lanham, political director of the Machinists. "We try to keep our communications open.... I think you can be professional enough to determine which issues you can work on and leave it at that." Boeing and the union have clashed over unemployment and workplace issues, but have worked together on health care, workers' compensation, and taxes, Lanham said. Such an attitude leaves Boeing less encumbered in the state legislature, where, many observers have concluded, the aerospace giant holds sway if not court.

5 / Paper Airplanes in the Marble Zoo

Boeing and the Legislature

An orangutan could lobby for the Boeing Company.
                              —Eleanor Lee, former state senator

It's all right to stand proudly upon ... and to decry the invisible
government. But it's the real government.
                              —William Allen White, 1924

BOEING'S QUEST for regulatory reform would have to go through the legislature. Once again, the company seemed well situated to get what it wanted. The building where they play for a lot of the marbles is, in fact, marble. And when the legislature is in session, staffers know the Capitol as "the marble zoo," for the antics of the members of its latest exhibit. By reputation, at least, Boeing is the weightiest ape, without parallel among the many interests who come calling during the four to six months the legislature is in session each year.

State Representative Jim Horn, a Republican and former Boeing manager, said most legislators easily grasp Boeing's importance. "When Boeing's employment is down, our state revenues are affected directly," he said (remember, once again, Sell's Third Law: *Economic interests will be politically dominant to the extent that they are economically dominant*). The official state revenue forecast always includes Boeing's payroll as a key component, Horn noted.

But Boeing is far from alone in the Capitol. Participants say Boeing is not the only aggressive force in the legislature. Agriculture, public employee unions, the University of Washington, and environmental interests display clout now and then, observers say. Former governor Dan Evans, who knew

Boeing's political power as well as anybody, said the company's image probably exceeded its reach: "I don't think Boeing gets what it wants all the time.... The legend gets built somewhat beyond reality. But they have been pretty good."

In Evans's estimation, aside from teachers and public employees, labor groups are not as powerful as they once were in Washington State. Environmental groups gained real power only in recent years, he said. The state's biggest business lobby, the Association of Washington Businesses, suffers from too broad a membership and hence an inability to coalesce around many issues. The state's largest firms, including Boeing and Weyerhaeuser, formed a Business Roundtable in the 1980s. "They do a pretty good job of analyzing public issues," Evans said, but the members tend to have divergent views on a number of issues. Still, Evans thinks the Roundtable is more influential than AWB within the state legislature.

The much smaller agricultural lobby always has been more powerful than other business lobbies, observers say. "They were united on anything that related to one portion of agriculture," Evans said. Eastern Washington legislators, although relatively small in number, could only gain by supporting their region's biggest employer. "What carried them over the top was that no urban legislator had any antipathy toward farmers. Everybody had to eat," he said. Moreover, farmers succeeded largely without paid lobbyists. "These were the guys themselves," Evans said of the farmers, who told tales of an industry that only a handful of legislators actually understood, since most were from cities and suburbs. "Business would be more effective if they'd send down a George Weyerhaeuser," Evans said.

Boeing does send top managers—rarely a Shrontz or a Condit, but usually someone fairly high up the food chain, with expertise in a particular subject matter. Rob Makin, Bud Coffey's successor as chief lobbyist in Olympia, said that between 1980 and 1994, he testified no more than three times before a legislative committee. "The luxury for us is that we've got somebody, someplace who knows about the company position," Makin said. "We'd rather have the experts testify. The company's got great people, bright people. They make very good witnesses." Those experts, in their rare appearances, draw crowds. When facilities vice-president Andy Gay ventured to Olympia to testify about the Everett affair (when the city sought more than $50 million to cover the cost of dealing with Boeing's 777 plant expansion), for example, the hearing room overflowed.

In Makin's estimation, "About four hundred people make politics in

Olympia work," including legislators, some staff, agency and department heads, and lobbyists. Business's rivals include what many in the capital know as the "Gang of Four"—public employee unions, teachers, trial lawyers, and the Washington State Labor Council, the local umbrella organization for the AFL-CIO. (It is not always a friendly competition, especially for some ardent conservatives: a labor council official who was appointed to fill a vacant legislative seat was absolutely shunned by some Republican legislators after she took office.)

While any number of legislators and other Boeing critics have charged the company with throwing its weight around, less passionate observers have concluded otherwise:

> The Boeing Co., perhaps because almost everyone realizes how synonymous its economic interests are with those of the state, fails to play the heavy role in legislative politics or campaign financing that oil, for instance, does in Texas, or coal in West Virginia, or copper until recent years in Montana. But while the company steers clear of exerting direct political influence commensurate with its power, it does have its lobbyists in Olympia, does run practical politics courses for its employees, and has encouraged scores of them to run successfully for public office.[1]

And those lobbyists and officials are busy. Like most large firms, Boeing has both macro and micro agendas, with the latter relating specifically to what Boeing wants for itself. "They go down [to Olympia] and they try to make their best case. That's what classic in-the-trenches lobbying has always been about," said Glenn Pascall, the economist and former revenue director. "There's no question that Boeing has a tax policy agenda. But do they always get what they want? No. Boeing's size and economic clout make it a very significant player. On the other hand, the very easy political mileage available to elected officials—who don't have strong ties to Boeing—is to stand up to Boeing."

Washington State relies largely on sales, property, and the gross-receipts business and occupations (B&O) tax. It is one of the few states without any kind of an income tax. As had happened several times before, in 1988 a state panel recommended tax reform, including some kind of an income tax.[2] Boeing opposed Governor Booth Gardner's subsequent tax reform proposal in 1989. "The current system has served the state well," the Boeing tax director Ray Otani told a legislative committee. "Let's make certain that any new system will serve our state and its citizens better." It is easy to conclude that Otani was disingenuous, but the particulars of the plan lend some support. The plan included a 4.1 percent corporate income tax, a 20 percent cut in the B&O, plus personal income taxes. The net result, however, was to shift state taxes from businesses to households (except, probably for Boeing, which could expect to pay more in income tax in good years than it would pay in B&O tax).[3] Nor is it sufficient to conclude that Boeing killed the tax; Gardner was an honest, well-intentioned, personally popular, and ineffectual governor, who was not particularly adept at working the political system.[4]

Boeing did oppose it, but they were hardly alone. "They were real strong advocates for maintaining the B&O tax," said one former state official. "Boeing certainly had the power to kill the package,... but the package was easily killable from a number of circles." On the other hand, the ex-official noted, Boeing was instrumental in helping the governor push through a fix when the federal courts invalidated how the state calculated the B&O tax paid by out-of-state firms.[5]

A Tacoma Democrat, State Representative Art Wang, said he was not out to "get Boeing" when he proposed a $524 million sales tax on component parts of aircraft. But the proposal went nowhere, despite the backing of a citizens group and the state teachers union, and despite control of both houses of the legislature and the governor's mansion by Wang's party, of which he was an influential member.[6] Of course, it probably didn't hurt Boeing's case to point to the $1.3 billion in state taxes it does pay every year.[7] Wang later claimed that Boeing blocked his appointment to a state pollution control board.[8]

Legislators who found themselves clashing with Boeing tended to be less than sanguine about the company's influence. "Boeing is the backbone of the state," said the longtime legislator and lobbyist Jolene Unsoeld. She battled the company over Superfund cleanup legislation in the late 1980s. "But that doesn't give them the license to screw the public.... We should be embarrassing the bejeebers out of an industry that claims what's good for them is good for the state."[9]

"They don't lobby, they don't testify," concurred Nancy Rust, then chairwoman of the House Environmental Affairs Committee. "They just kill things."[10] But despite Unsoeld's account of the Superfund battle, it is not clear that Boeing alone was the bill's undoing. Other businesses held the same position as Boeing, and it is not all that remarkable that Republican legislators who generally support business were inclined to vote no.[11]

One does not find traces of jet fuel wherever Boeing has been. While it usually prevails in tax matters, on matters such as liability limitations, where the also-powerful trial lawyers weigh in, Boeing sometimes loses. Nor does Boeing watch everything that happens under the Capitol dome. Pascall said Boeing is to some extent preoccupied with its product rather than with politics. "It really is run by engineers and people who make the product. It is not run by corporate attorneys. They don't play politics at the grand level quite to the degree that their size would suggest."

"They've learned over the years to choose their fights and choose them carefully and not engage in any more than they have to," said the former Boeing employee and state senator Gary Grant. Issues that have a direct impact on Boeing get attention; those that do not are left alone. Others see Boeing taking a wide approach on what is important to the company. "They tend to take a pretty broad view of what their interests are," said one former legislator who faced dogfights with Boeing on a number of topics. Dan Grimm, former state treasurer and House Ways and Means Committee chairman, said Boeing has gotten most of what it wants out of the state. "They are the single most important element as far as the development of public policy in the state," he said. "That's merely a recognition of their role in the state's economy."

Part of political influence is backing it up with campaign contributions. Over time, Boeing's contributions have grown. For a long time, Boeing spent surprisingly little on campaign contributions (though relatively more on money given directly to parties and formal interest groups). In 1980–81, Walfred H. Peterson conducted a survey in which manufacturers, which largely means Boeing, ranked only seventh in terms of campaign contributions; in his survey for 1982, legislators ranked Boeing fifth in terms of legislative influence and eighth in terms of campaign influence.[12]

Up until the 1960s, Boeing gave very little money to candidates, and the amount rose but little up to 1980. For several years thereafter, Boeing ranked somewhere down the list of big-time contributors to state-level candidates. Coffey convinced the company to get more actively involved. Now local and state candidates are reviewed and agreed to by the Board of Directors each year. By the mid-1990s, Boeing's total contribution placed it in the upper echelon of state political interests. The state Public Disclosure Commission's somewhat haphazard pattern of reporting contributions makes it hard to say precisely where. Walker placed Boeing seventh in 1990 (although including lobbying expenses, manufacturers ranked anywhere from first to third).[13]

A recent campaign finance reform limited the size of all donations; Boeing's response was to give more money to ancillary political action committees. "We don't direct them, but we trust them," said Makin, Coffey's immediate successor. Boeing shunned independent expenditures in legislative races, he said. Opposition legislators liked to complain that Boeing owned and operated some prominent business lobbying groups, such as United for Washington and the Association of Washington Businesses, but the size of the company's contributions, at least as reported to the disclosure commission, does not support such criticism.

Having enough money certainly is essential to getting elected.[14] But even before reforms limited the size of contributions to legislative races, a typical race involved dozens if not hundreds of contributors for each candidate. And money will go only so far to achieve desired outcomes. "It's hard to change the dynamics of an election with money when you can't put much money in," Coffey said. Boeing rarely ever gave more than a few thousand dollars to any legislative candidate, even in the prereform days when it could do so. Moreover, United for Washington did not actually dump large contributions into very many races itself. Campaign contributions will no longer seal any deal, Makin said. "At $500 a shot, who cares? You've got to have a good story or it doesn't go."

Boeing's campaign contributions were spread out for maximum influence, to open doors as much as anything. Even some candidates who rarely supported Boeing got money, Makin said. The company made campaign contributions to legislative and local candidates, as well as to county and state party organizations.

"If you get the right people elected," things are smoother, Coffey said. "We spend a lot of time trying to sort out candidates." They looked for common and economic sense, he said. The contributions help counter union and public employee support, Coffey added. "You get a line drawn there which is really unfortunate," between candidates with pro- and anti-union sympathies.

Boeing undoubtedly does not spend more because (A) it does not have to and (B) to do so would be to come on too strongly. And besides, money does not always buy love or results. Located so close to Alaska, the state has five major oil refineries. Although the oil companies have spent a lot in campaign contributions (often ranking at or near the top), that has not saved them from substantial regulation, former governor Evans noted. (For example, oil industry officials were complaining in 1997 that Washington had the toughest tanker restrictions in the country.)

Boeing, on the other hand, has something to show for its efforts. Following a similar move in California on behalf of Douglas Aircraft Corporation, the state of Washington in the 1960s granted a sales tax exemption on aircraft and parts. The state's chief remaining business tax, the business and occupations tax, is a tax on gross receipts. Despite years of complaints from small firms and start-ups that they pay the B&O regardless of whether they are making any money, it remains unchanged. For a big company such as Boeing, the advantage of the B&O is that it does not change no matter how strong profits are. In the early 1980s, Boeing helped kill the state's inventory tax, which was being levied on aircraft awaiting delivery. Boeing also manages its own industrial insurance fund, no doubt at considerable savings to itself.

"We are quite active in tax reform," Coffey said in 1976. "If Boeing had to pay a 5 percent sales tax on the planes sold, we couldn't compete in the market and [would] have to move out of Washington."[15] The state's tax code "was pretty much written to accommodate Boeing and written around the specific situations that affect Boeing," said State Treasurer Grimm. He added that as "someone who has tangled with Boeing on occasion," he did not find that "necessarily wrong."

Boeing sometimes does flex its political pectorals. In June 1987, corporate raider T. Boone Pickens announced he intended to acquire 15 percent of Boeing's shares[16] (federal securities regulations require anyone to make such an announcement anytime her or his holdings go above 5 percent of a single company). Pickens never said what he was hoping for, but Boeing took the threat seriously after the investor sent a letter informing the company he planned to buy 2 percent of Boeing's stock. Company officials feared that Pickens would put Boeing "into play," and with a low stock price, low earnings, and $3 billion in cash, Boeing was a natural takeover target.[17] Ford was rumored to be considering a takeover bid as well.[18] "People who had never blinked before were shaking in their shoes," one first-hand observer recalled.

Shrontz got the board of directors to pass an antitakeover plan. Boeing then turned to government, lining up support in Washington, D.C., even as it worked to get help from Olympia.[19] The bill that Boeing wanted would have barred significant asset sales (a favorite tactic for funding leveraged buyouts) for five years without board approval in advance of the takeover.[20] It applied only to companies with more than 20,000 employees, which at that point was a set of one. The Machinists Union, meanwhile, pushed for an amendment that would include a severance package for laid-off employees, which Boeing opposed.[21] Legislators also hinted at trading the takeover bill for Boeing support of environmental and tax reform bills, which Coffey said Boeing would not agree to.[22] Boeing continued to lobby; Shrontz went to Olympia to meet with the governor and legislative leaders on July 30.[23] Ultimately, Governor Booth Gardner called a special session, to fix a court-voided portion of the state's business and occupations tax, and to help Boeing.[24]

After a mere two weeks in the valley of dearth, Boeing got its bill in early August. It passed 44 to 2 in the state senate and 77 to 12 in the house, without the union-backed severance package. Boeing compromised by agreeing to a proviso barring more than 5 percent layoffs at a company that had been taken over.[25] Opponents of the measure tended to be those on either the far right or the far left.[26] "Even legislators who see a Boeing trick behind every move the company makes—and there are a number of them—don't want the company hurt," Layton concluded.[27]

Although Rodgers concluded that "Boeing is a loner in Olympia,"[28] that is not what first-hand observers say. Boeing multiplies its clout and masks its presence by building coalitions with like-minded interests. "They kind of head up the business lobby in Olympia. They call the shots out of that lobby," said a former legislator and lobbyist. He added that Boeing "pretty effectively controls" United for Washington, a major business political action committee.

Boeing was very good at building coalitions, Evans said. Boeing lobbyists, led by Bud Coffey, worked behind the scenes or out in front as required. "They built their reputation for power," he said. "Every time you have a success, you build reputation. The reputation builds up and impresses newcomers. They are then less likely to say, 'I'm going to take them on.'" "I recall beating AWB [the Association of Washington Businesses, the state's largest business lobby] on many occasions," said former state senator Grant. "I'm not sure I beat the Boeing Company very often by themselves." "When there was something in the legislature that they didn't want, it just sort of didn't happen," said former Everett mayor Pete Kinch. Boeing's tactics were never very complicated, however. Coffey said he simply tried to communicate well and bring reliable information to legislators.[29]

At times, Boeing is drawn into politics without previously having expressed interest. In 1970, Governor Evans offered up a plan that would have put a lid on the property tax, repealed the gross-revenues business and occupations tax, and substituted a flat-rate personal income tax (the flat rate being required by the terms of the state constitution, which requires equal taxation for all forms of property, including money). In 1973, he got a graduated income tax on the ballot, complete with constitutional amendment. Both measures failed. One used to hear speculation that Boeing had pulled strings to ground one or the other of the ballot measures, but Evans blamed recession and fear. He called on T. Wilson to lead the 1973 campaign. "He was out in front for it," Evans said. Weyerhaeuser, the gigantic timber company, opposed the measure. "Weyerhaeuser was high profit margin; Boeing was high volume and low margin," Evans explained. "The business community was split up."

Evans said he chose Wilson to lead the campaign because "he was powerful enough and gutsy enough. His voice was important because he was chairman of Boeing." On the surface, Wilson was a dour and taciturn figure, who nonetheless guided Boeing through its dire days in the early 1970s and long remained beloved by many employees. Although he took some heat from his colleagues in executive circles, "none of his business associates would take him on too hard," Evans said. "He wouldn't just sit back and take it." Wilson, Boeing, and other large firms later opposed an initiative to create a corporate profits tax, however.[30]

Local journalists, such as Doug Underwood,[31] usually have concluded that Boeing gets what it wants from the state. Dick Larsen, a longtime *Seattle Times* legislative reporter, said Boeing was not obvious in its efforts, however. "Boeing power was always more implicit than explicit," he said. "A lot of it is aura, whether they really exert it or not."

Pascall said the company's clout was not exaggerated. "Boeing is the 800-pound gorilla and the answer is yes," he said. But the company has long been aware of that status and feared a backlash if it took advantage of its position. "Especially Bud Coffey was cognizant of the need to pick his shots on the issues. Boeing just couldn't blow into town all the time and flex its muscles on any issue that it wants."

Boeing's lobbyists are "very effective," said Linda Lanham, a lobbyist for the Machinists. "They understand all aspects of legislation. They do their research and they have great negotiating skills." State Representative Horn, a former Boeing engineer, said he had received no complaints about Boeing's lobbying efforts from other legislators (who, it should be added, are not averse to complaining long and loud if it suits them). The company did not "come in and thump its fist on the table," Larsen said. Boeing lobbyists, over the years, have tended to be somewhat restrained. "They want to avoid the appearance of strong-arming." And they have been, by all accounts, scrupulously honest. Chairman William Allen once instructed his lobbyists, "Don't do anything you wouldn't want to read on the front page of the paper or have to lie about under oath."[32]

Another advantage for Boeing's lobbyists has been having the trust of their employer, Grimm said. "They were given the discretion to exercise judgment in Olympia," he said. "They didn't have to get into discussions about end-game compromises. I think that gives them great credibility in a political environment. A lot of lobbyists are simply couriers." Armed with that kind of trust, company officials were effectively insulated from legislators. "I was never able to go around them," a former top legislative leader said of Coffey and his minions. "A call to Shrontz or anybody in the company was invariably returned by Bud."

At the start and the heart of Boeing's legislative power was Forrest G. "Bud" Coffey, one of the most remarkable men ever to work in Washington State politics. Tall, dignified, usually soft-spoken, Coffey might be mistaken for the corner optometrist except for an unusual sharpness of gaze. Behind the calm demeanor, however, things always seemed to be moving. Coffey never seemed to be not at work, whether at a reception for legislative staffers at his Black Lake home near Olympia, or cruising the halls of the Marble Zoo.

Coffey set the standard, holding the throttle on Boeing's legislative efforts from 1971 to 1995, and eventually picking and grooming his successors. He started out working in the company's Washington, D.C., office, then moved to Olympia in 1971, when Boeing executives decided their home-state lobbyists were too far right for the company's best interests.[33] He was, by all accounts, a man with deceptive charms and a man to be reckoned with.

"Bud's a pretty smooth operator," said Larsen. "He keeps an eye on everything political. He's a very good handicapper." "He knew when to push and when not to push," said former Seattle mayor Wes Uhlman. "In other cities where you have one large employer there's a great deal of tension and sometimes outright war. The tension will always be there but there's never been a war. Puget Sound politics has been nice and Bud is a nice person. He fit into that rather well." "Bud was easy to communicate with," said Lanham. "Bud would just talk to anybody. He was always willing to listen." "Bud is the epitome of the corporate diplomat," Pascall said. "When I joined Dan Evans's staff as his legislative assistant [in the early 1970s], the first person who noticed and dropped by to pay a personal call was Bud Coffey." "He's very solicitous of secretarial staff," Larsen noted—a practice that can get you where you need to be in the state capital.

Once there, Coffey and his minions knew what to do. "They were very good at presenting their case one-on-one with legislators," said one former state official. Evans said Coffey made the most of what he had. "Bud was very able in his own right," he said. "He counseled his corporate bosses that you don't waste your ammunition on everything. That's a tough act to follow. He just had a very good way with people. He had muscle because of who he represented, but he gained muscle over time." "Bud Coffey is without equal," said former state senator Grant. "Bud paid his dues," said his successor as Boeing vice-president for government affairs, John Hayden. "He had credibility. People thought he was an honest broker. For a long time, he was the only voice of the Boeing Company."

Up until his retirement in 1996, Coffey rarely actually testified at a legislative hearing, and he would not consent to interviews with journalists unless he was caught on the fly. Boeing officials say they prefer to use appropriate experts when necessary; the manager in charge of taxes will testify on a tax bill; a public relations person will talk to a reporter. Then again, others say, in the case of Coffey, he did not have to say much in public. One former suburban official, asked about various other prominent lobbyists, acknowledged that they were powerful, but still not in Coffey's class. "Bud doesn't have to testify. He makes a phone call." Although Coffey was very gracious and charming, the ex-official said, it was a phone call you didn't want to get. Speaking of one of Boeing's suburban lobbyists, he added, "If Paul Seeley calls you, that's interesting. If Terry Lewis [Seeley's boss] calls you, that's more interesting; you should probably call him back. If Bud Coffey calls you, take two Tylenol. The shit has hit the fan."

"He was very candid with me," agreed Shinpoch, the former legislator, Boeing manager, and state agency director. As a Democrat, Shinpoch was not always on the same side of the aisle as business or Boeing. "If you weren't going to like the answer, you didn't ask him the question." "Coffey can get in to see the governor quicker than a legislative leader can," said one rival lobbyist.[34] Former house speaker Joe King expressed frustration at not being able to "smoke out" Coffey and his cadres on some important issues, but added, "To the best of my knowledge they've never tried to mislead me, never lied to me."[35] Dan Grimm said Coffey was skillful, but that being from Boeing did not hurt. "Anyone who has the portfolio from Boeing is a player," he said. "Rob Makin has the same portfolio and has the same access to people Bud Coffey did."

Coffey, in a rare interview, was predictably modest about the company's clout. "We're given a lot more credit for power than we really have," he said. Still, it was Coffey to whom public and private officials turned to help build coalitions to keep the Seahawks and Mariners in Seattle, and it was to Coffey that Shrontz turned for both education reform and United Way fund-raising. "He's a hard man to say no to," confided another official involved with United Way, after a cup of Coffey. "He's got us hopping."

Coffey said Boeing tried to play the political game by accounting for the diverse demands that most elected officials face. "We spend a lot of time trying to understand," he said. The company's lobbyists work year-round, "having a presence." Still, he added, "We rarely push an issue hard." Boeing relied on making its case "on its merits." Coffey said Boeing tried hard to be bipartisan in its political initiatives (which only makes sense in a competitive, two-party state). "We try to never let it be personal," he said. "We work very hard on credibility and good visibility. We have almost unlimited access. It's rare when I can't see anybody I want to see. But if you're not credible, you lose it in a hurry."

Coffey also brought up a troop of quality lobbyists behind him, from Rob Makin and Al Ralston to a squadron of local government lobbyists scattered around Puget Sound. All were competent and smooth without being the least bit oily or unctuous, well versed in the arguments and ideas that make up the world according to Boeing. Although Hayden was brought in from Boeing's D.C. office to replace Coffey in 1995, Makin long appeared to be the heir apparent. Physically, Makin has a different book jacket from Coffey's: he is shorter, dark-haired, stylish, and wiry, in contrast to Coffey's easy Southern grace. But the pages read the same. Despite the GQ exterior, Makin was at once just as charming and relaxed as Coffey. Observers say Makin and Ralston were not above playing good cop/bad cop in the legislature. Makin, however, was described as more of a streetfighter, a man with a taste for the hand-to-hand combat of legislative politics. Ralston looked less refined and appeared more affable, but both were described as razor-sharp.

Coffey's successors learned their lessons well, observers said. "I never in all the years I've been in Olympia had Bud Coffey or Rob Makin say anything to me that was even in error, let alone being subject to interpretation," Grimm said. "Rob is very smart but he has a much more trench-warrior style than Bud. He likes to win and sometimes he likes to take no prisoners." But their approach was never personal, Grimm added. "Bud inculcated in Rob Makin a sense of 'never think of legislators as a friend or an enemy; think of them as allies and opponents.' It's a much more dispassionate approach."

Doug Levy, a lobbyist for the city of Everett, knew Ralston from the latter's days working for the city of Seattle. "Al Ralston's good because he's good," Levy said. "I think he has the ability to disagree with a legislator or a lobbyist and be able to shake hands and say so and not antagonize them. That's a real admirable trait." One observer called Makin and Ralston "the bomb-thrower and the diplomat." He added, "If Rob or Al want to see a legislator on the floor, they see him. If Boeing wants to go to the mat for an issue, they get the issue. It's daunting." "They brought in Al for some Democratic ties, but Rob calls the shots," said one former legislator.

Makin and Ralston said they built their success on personal relationships as well as expert testimony, with each maneuver reinforcing the other. "It lets them [legislators] know the company has a policy approach to our political positions," Makin said. "Personal relationships allow you to move a lot of information fast. There's strength in employment numbers but also in information. In that [legislative] process, information is power. Our job is both to advocate for the company, but we're also consultants to the company." "We bring a lot of information to the company," Ralston added.

"Our only agenda is the competitiveness of The Boeing Co.," Makin said. "We try to never, ever let it get personal, so that the people that you're fighting with are your friends next time." A handful of legislators do dislike Boeing, he said. "I've had some pretty ferocious fights on issues, but we've stayed friends." Like Coffey, Makin and Ralston ignored almost no one. "We spend a lot of time with back-benchers," Ralston said. "They're the leaders in a couple of years." Election victors will get communication from Boeing from the outset, "to discuss what's desired and what's possible," Makin said.

Although they tended to downplay their accomplishments, the lobbyists admitted that the company, as a whole, was successful in Olympia. It was not a given, however, Makin said, hinting at "big companies with marginal to pathetic public affairs" efforts. "We've done very well under D administrations and D majorities," Makin said, using the Capitol shorthand for Democrat. Still, by the mid-1990s, they were less than satisfied with the overall results. "The legislature rarely adjourns having made the Boeing Company more competitive," Makin said. "We have not done as good a job as I hope we do in the future of focusing the legislature on our overall competition," Ralston said. "Airbus is a good focal point. If we lose market share, we'll get tougher down there or we'll leave the state."

Although Coffey could admit that Boeing's lobbyists spent most of their time trying to keep things from happening to the company, for Boeing, ultimately, the task was to goad government into some degree of predictability. "Our fundamental philosophy is that well-run government benefits the Boeing Company," Coffey said. "Dysfunctional government serves people who don't want things to happen. We want things to happen." It is hard to imagine that what they wanted to happen was growth management, Washington style. The company's litany of complaints about dealing with state and local government is ample testimony to that.

The preceding two chapters should make clear that Boeing has done nearly everything it could to account for Sell's Second Law. The company not only builds good products, it has built an image and a sociopolitical program second to none. Boeing has left almost nothing to chance. But what should not be forgotten amid all the toasts to Boeing's size and political skill is that despite an admirable public affairs effort, despite the company's unparalleled economic footprint, it was not able to shunt the inexorable advance of the Paradox of Growth.

6 / Things Happen

A Tale of Several Cities

Nobody's rolling over and playing dead for business.
—Jay Covington, Renton city administrator

BOEING'S THREATS TO LEAVE were felt keenly in the cities where its plants reside. Renton and Everett in particular had become nearly synonymous with Boeing, so great was the company's presence in those two towns. And it was in the cities where the Paradox of Growth, in the form of the Growth Management Act, was most felt by all the players. Ultimately it was Boeing's experience with the cities that drove Frank Shrontz to threaten to move new production away.

From the start, Boeing had hung on to Seattle firmly and at arm's length. While its headquarters are just inside the city limits, most of its original Duwamish-area facilities are just outside of Seattle. The company kept its Spartan headquarters amid the industrial squalor of the Duwamish corridor—and not in a downtown high-rise—in part to keep a lower profile around town.[1]

For a long time, as Edward C. Banfield noted, Seattle city politics were on the woolly side:

In the 1930s Seattle was probably the widest open port in the country. Its politicians were always flamboyant and often corrupt.... The city had a tradition of labor radicalism and popular discontent; elections were bitterly fought along class lines, and incumbents usually lost.[2]

It was, at a minimum, all the more reason for Boeing to stay just beyond Seattle's reach. At one point, the city went so far as to gerrymander its southern border to keep Boeing happily outside of the city limits.[3] But the company and the city have become inextricably linked:

> The union of Boeing and Seattle is like some marriages. One partner is pretty, the other a stalwart breadwinner. They're proud of their spouses, usually tolerate each other's faults, and fight and make up every so often. For the most part they feel comfortable together and would rather have the other as a mate than not.[4]

The company understood the relationship and what it meant to the region. "Even when our plants are going at top speed, it was never comfortable to feel that Boeing was responsible for so much of the area's progress and prosperity. It was not a healthy situation," one executive said.[5]

And when those plants are going full bore, the dollar signs tend to light up in public officials' eyes. Scott Johnson cites five distinct attempts by Seattle to annex the South Park neighborhood and, with it, Boeing's enviable tax base. The company turned back each attempt until smaller and more pliable Tukwila annexed the area in 1989.[6] Boeing dodged Seattle, confirmed Terry Lewis, its chief municipal government liaison. "We activated the South Park community, and they turned it around for us," he said. Using the offices of Gogerty and Stark, a well-connected local public affairs firm, Boeing engineered annexation by Tukwila, where the government was less inclined, in Boeing's eyes, to milk the company for fun and profit.

Bob Gogerty had been deputy mayor under Wes Uhlman. After Uhlman did not seek re-election, he was replaced by Charlie Royer, a former television journalist, and Gogerty went into public affairs. Royer was determined to get more Boeing property onto the city's tax rolls. "Bob was very successful in holding Charlie off," said Uhlman, who tried and failed to annex "the Boeing pocket" himself in 1974. (Boeing did once look at moving its corporate headquarters to a site just west of Seattle-Tacoma International Airport. Nearby residents opposed their would-be neighbor, however, and stalled the project until Boeing changed its mind.)[7]

Even at the municipal level, Boeing leaves little to chance, recruiting top talent to work the cities. Terry Lewis left the banking business to become a lobbyist for Boeing in 1980, rising to the rank of corporate director for local government affairs. Under Lewis, Paul Seeley managed South King County public affairs, including Boeing's plants in the cities of Auburn, Kent, and

Renton. In Everett, Boeing's affairs were watched by Frank Figg. Both men got excellent reviews from the city officials with whom they worked, and both were regular fixtures at chamber meetings, public hearings, and quasi-social gatherings.

In Everett, for example, they thought highly of Frank Figg. "I think that Everett is lucky that Boeing has someone who is charged with keeping in close touch with Everett," said Doug Levy, an ex-journalist who became the city's chief lobbyist. "Frank is clearly well integrated into the community. They want to be well represented in the community, and I think that probably there is a community expectation that Boeing should be a player in the community." City officials also enjoy the added clout Boeing can bring to intergovernmental negotiations. "I'm convinced we'll get a lot farther having Boeing and their lobbying clout in D.C. There are times when it's to our advantage to have them," said Jay Covington, Renton city administrator.

For Boeing, the cities are facts of business life that cannot be ignored. Like all Boeing public affairs commandos, the Lewis trio was assigned the task of keeping costs down wherever possible. "If we can cut a permit process from eighteen to six months, we've saved ourselves some money," Lewis explained. Boeing's process for local government is according to blueprint: identify issues, find allies, build relationships with key staff people and elected officials. That includes keeping local government officials informed when employment is going to surge or ebb. When Shrontz took over as chairman, he decided that Boeing had been too secretive, which tended to foster some suspicion and mistrust of the company in the region. But even before Shrontz's civic glasnost, Boeing spent company funds on public affairs courses for employees, to get them involved—and the company represented—in civic life.[8] One journalist observed, "You go anywhere where there is any type of activity going on and by the very weight of these people, Boeing controls Seattle."[9]

Lewis said the company is not completely unconscious of its clout. "Yes, we have power," he said. "Do we try to use it? We try not to. We're so sensitive that we don't use it to our advantage. Does it open doors? Yes. Does it give us our way anytime we want to use it? No. Nor should it. That's the system. We certainly don't want to abuse it."

Still, the company is not always successful. Fire codes in one location required Boeing to build an enclosed, indoor escape passage in the middle of a large manufacturing plant. "Common sense says you're not going to get in an enclosed space if there's a fire," Lewis said. But at least one former city official, who generally praised Boeing's approach to municipal relations, said the company's internal inertia did not help such processes. "They have to go through more levels than anybody," the official said. "Boeing has the biggest bureaucracy in the state." One permit took twelve months to acquire. "In this 12 months, seven of it was on their side of the coin."

Nonetheless, Boeing officials said they were not getting much home-field advantage in working in and around Seattle. "Puget Sound generally has a no-growth attitude," said Doug Beighle, a Boeing senior vice-president, speaking at yet another economic development conference in 1993. "Growth is regarded as a burden, not a benefit." He was quick to point out what that meant to Boeing. "For almost two months I drove by an open ditch on East Marginal Way. We couldn't get a building inspector out so we couldn't finish building a curb." The permitting process took twenty-eight months at the Duwamish site, eighteen months at Everett, "and we're still hung up at Longacres."

The Integrated Aircraft Systems Laboratory, in which Boeing engineers can rigorously test working components of aircraft under design, and the Duwamish land on which it sits became something of a battleground for Boeing and Seattle. Boeing rejected the area as a site for a new wind tunnel, because of concerns over getting adequate electric power as well as the environmental and construction permit processes. The test lab itself was further delayed by conflicting information from the environmental and engineering sections of Seattle City Light. The topper for Boeing came when a City Light official locked a key document in his desk and then went on vacation for three weeks. Boeing figured the total four-month delay cost them about $1 million. Beighle said the adventure was "indicative of an attitude of indifference and disregard for the applicant's need for timely decisions."[10]

Boeing, like any good business, just wanted a little predictability. "As long as we know the rule of the road and get early determination, that will go a long way to let us plan our actions accordingly," said John Hayden, Bud Coffey's successor as vice-president for government affairs. "We're wasting a lot of time, money, and effort because of this myriad of bureaucracy that has to be dealt with."

But the incident is also indicative of the Paradox of Growth. However cumbersome the process, it did not arise spontaneously. The sometimes labyrinthine regulations, the interminable permit polka, and the apparent lack of concern (which on the inside must appear as painstaking carefulness), all came in response to growth, and in response to longstanding public demands to manage it. But the Paradox is rarely a matter of public policy debate. Certainly nobody inside of Boeing seemed to recognize it, and few others outside the company seemed to have any inkling of the bigger forces at play.

Boeing's approach to dealing with the cities was similar to how it worked in the legislature: careful and relatively low-key (at least until company officials started their litany of public complaints). Despite their apparent unhappiness with the civic state of affairs, Boeing officials never played rough, local observers said. "They don't often swing their weight around inordinately," said one former local official. "If you abuse that potential [power], you lose credibility. They are very cautious about using their influence." "They're all very credible and very professional people in how they did business," said another former Everett mayor, Peter Kinch. "They would never come and try to strong-arm us. They would come and express their point of view. The [city] council was very reluctant to get crossways with Boeing. Once in a while they did." As a consequence, the city gave Boeing a tax break on a special levy to build a new minor-league baseball park. "We could have forced them, but you want to think about that. That may not be where you want to burn a chip," Kinch said.

The relationships were built over time, as neither Renton nor Everett had recruited Boeing to come there. And as with Puget Sound in general, Boeing landed in those towns at least partly by chance.

RENTON

In some ways, Renton is not where one would expect to find an airplane factory. Boeing's plant sits on prime real estate, where the Cedar River winds into Lake Washington; homes on other parts of the lake, with views not remarkably better, sell for $500,000 and up. It is on Lake Washington, for example, that Bill Gates built his massive, mostly underground compound.

But without runways, water was what launched airplanes in the early days, so the site was a natural. The Renton location was first developed by Boeing test pilot Eddie Hubbard in 1919 so that he could launch seaplanes from the lake. Hubbard and Bill Boeing made the first international mail flight, from Seattle to Canada, in that year, and Hubbard flew the mail for eight years. The sight of aircraft regularly skimming off the lake gave people the idea that it was OK to fly, according to Morda Slauson.[11]

When the Navy wanted seaplanes for World War II, the Renton site became a factory. Only one flying boat was built there, but the plant soon was turning out B-29s. The war and Boeing changed Renton from a small mining town of 4,000 people to "a congested and busy industrial center,"[12] with a population of around 40,000. Boeing did not actually buy the site from the government until 1962, but by then it was the jet capital of the world.

An airport that could handle jets, Renton Municipal Airport, grew up next to the plant, which eventually let Boeing build its first jetliners in Renton. The always-working-class town, which got its start with coal and lumber, stayed that way. So many people worked in Renton that its daytime population was (and is) double its nighttime census—at least 40,000 people come to work in Renton every day. Depending on current production rates, Boeing employs around 25,000 people in Renton, or about 59 percent of all Renton jobs, making it by far the city's largest employer.

Boeing came to signify Renton if not to dominate it. "I'm beginning to think we should change our name to Boeington," said one longtime resident (not a bad thought, since Bill Boeing was known to have visited, while it is doubtful that Captain William Renton ever saw the place). "We're completely dominated by Boeing. But, of course, we're grateful."[13]

The Renton plant usually is busy. Even with lower production rates during down cycles, churning out 707, 727, 737, and 757 models has kept the plant occupied if not always at capacity. The lack of room eventually drove Boeing to expand in Everett, and spurred the company to squeeze every spare inch of space it could at the Renton site itself. The issue came to a head in the late 1980s and early 1990s, when Boeing planned a $430 million redevelopment of the Renton plant to accommodate ramped-up production of 737 and 757 models.

For the company, the issue was getting permits quickly enough to expedite its construction work. For the city, however, the issue was quite different: how to pay for infrastructure needs that would be generated by Boeing's expansion. In other words, the Paradox of Growth: Renton could not just say no to Boeing, but it had to find a way to accommodate growth's externalities. "In the late '80s there was so much growth happening that it was a defense reaction," said Jay Covington, Renton city administrator.

Added manufacturing capacity at Boeing would mean more jobs, and some added revenue through a head tax. But most of the city's revenue comes from sales tax. Washington State has the second highest sales tax in the nation, and perhaps no other state is as dependent on this source of funds. It is certainly true for Washington cities. Riddled with retail, much smaller and nearby Tukwila is awash in cash, whereas larger, industrial Renton generally scrapes by. "Our tax structure sucks; it's awful," Covington said. "Those engineers make good money. We don't see any of it unless they spend it in our town. Our cash cows are IKEA (a home-furnishings store), and the cinema complex. But they pay retail-wage jobs."

Nor could the city make loans to the company to help it pay for mitigation; the state constitution prohibits extending public credit to private enterprises except by port districts. (No one apparently thought to bring in the Port of Seattle; port districts are specifically cited in the state constitution as the government of choice for aiding economic development. The port did eventually approach Boeing to see if it could help with its land needs.)

Renton implemented a per-person "head tax" on workers in 1988, raising $1.8 million a year. It sold the tax to business by promising to use the money to leverage federal grants and make transportation improvements. "We push for manufacturing-wage jobs, but what you get out of manufacturing is property tax and utility tax," Covington said. The property tax raises about $10 million for the city, the utility tax much less. Renton would have to ask Boeing for help in coping with the plant expansion. Boeing wanted quick approval from the city, and agreed to pay for hiring extra staff to expedite permits.[14]

The North Renton neighborhood, a flat pasture of smallish, postwar, single-family homes and carefully drawn streets, is tucked all around the Boeing plant on three sides (Lake Washington is on the fourth). This is old Renton, the original town, where a lot of Boeing people once lived. By the time of the expansion, however, a number of the residents had reached retirement age, and expansion of anything had taken a back seat to quality-of-life issues.

To get permits, Boeing agreed to a number of conditions, including changing engine test times and installing cautionary signs along a nearby trail along the Cedar River.[15] It also agreed to pay the city close to $2 million to mitigate traffic and noise concerns. The mitigation package included donating land and a boathouse to extend the Cedar River Trail, and paying to build the trail itself; developing a transportation management plan; contributing $820,000 for street improvements in North Renton; and working to find ways to cut air pollution from painting and cleaning operations.[16]

A citizens' group, concerned about traffic and airport noise, formed to question if not oppose the project. Boeing and the city agreed to study the issues, and a panel was convened. The group, the North Renton–Kennydale Neighborhood Defense Fund, had previously sued the city over its handling of construction of a couple of Boeing office towers. The group was most concerned about what impact Boeing expansion would have on housing values.[17] Although Boeing pledged $200,000 to implement noise improvements recommended by the citizens' panel, the panel could not find a solution that left it completely happy. Wherever Boeing tested jet engines, someone was going to be inconvenienced, it seemed.[18] Neighborhood opposition did convince Boeing not to move its engine testing to the west side of Renton Airport, however.[19] A panel of city officials eventually decided that the project was so important as to overwhelm the noise concerns.[20] The citizens' group complained, and the City Council listened, and instructed city staff to find a better solution to the noise problem. In particular, Boeing wanted leeway to test engines at noon, when the river trail is usually at its busiest.[21] The city and Boeing eventually agreed on a final version, and the citizens group was quieted if not satisfied. Appeals of the expansion permits were filed and denied, and some fell by the wayside because of errors in filings.

Boeing pressed on. Renton Boeing general manager Jim Johnson explained the company's position at a Chamber of Commerce luncheon: a booming market meant output had to be boosted or sales would be lost. "We must expand our production capacity or we will lose our markets," Johnson said. But he praised the city for its cooperation and assured the business folk, "We plan to be here for a long, long time. We want to be a good neighbor and a good business associate."[22]

But Boeing also was wrestling with the county's transportation utility, Metro, "which insisted we charge our employees for parking to force them into bus and van service which Metro was unable to provide," Beighle later said. Metro's service did not quite reach Boeing's plants. Concerns over fire protection forced the company to spend $500,000 to put in a second water main. Beighle characterized Renton at that time as "a difficult neighborhood environment that expected all problems of the past to be cured with this project."

Amidst all this, an unlikely opponent waded into the fray. Sanford "Sandy" Webb was a Renton resident, a perennial and unsuccessful candidate for city office, and a Boeing engineer. He was the kind of man noted for referring to himself in the third person in his frequent letters to the editor at *Valley Daily News*, but he was not without his share of sympathizers. Webb said the city had not imposed sufficient conditions on the project, a position with which some citizens and at least one city councilman agreed.[23] Boeing was smart enough or unconcerned enough to leave its in-house gadfly largely alone, and the usually vociferous Webb never complained about the company harassing him for his efforts. But Webb was denied at every turn, before city hearing examiners and in court. Boeing's frustration, due to be magnified a few years later when it pursued expansion of its Longacres project, was that anyone could file an appeal and hold up a project for weeks if not months, raising the company's legal costs and delaying construction.

Despite the initial haggling, Renton mayor Earl Clymer instructed city staff to expedite Boeing's expansion permits, and the City Council hired extra police and fire personnel in expectation of additional revenue. But the end of the Cold War and the down cycle in the aircraft business led Boeing to scale back its expansion by April 1990,[24] and the city budget suffered as a result. Boeing's planned payments to the city fell from $2 million to $1.47 million.[25] Layoffs followed, leading some to criticize the city for jumping too quickly at Boeing's call.[26]

But, Covington said, realistically, the city could do little other than try to help its largest employer. "In this state, business pays the bills," to the tune of 70 to 80 percent of tax collections, he said. "You've got to pay attention to them. If they leave, you're in trouble. There was a real concern that Boeing could be vulnerable. We were looking at losing 10 to 15,000 employees. I think the council realized that. We wanted to take as much action as we could. We wanted to let them know that there was no reason for them go somewhere else and spend a bunch of money."

When Boeing began working on a new family of derivatives for its popular 737 line, city officials intervened again, meeting weekly with company officials to smooth out the wrinkles in renewed expansion and refurbishment of the Renton plant. "They've got deadlines and they've got to get planes out," Covington said. "We've said, 'You're here, you've got a facility, and we've tried to help you with this. Let's work together.' They've responded to that. There's been a pretty good partnership philosophy mostly in the last three to four years."

But it was not just the city that Boeing had to wrestle with. The state Department of Transportation originally said Boeing should pay to add freeway lanes to Interstate 405 and State Route 167. Boeing built neither, but did end up building the Oakesdale Avenue extension, and then turned it over to the city. "Boeing has stepped up to the plate as a corporate citizen," Covington said.

The company's citizenship was to be tested over the next few years, however. In 1989, Boeing found itself in the horse-racing business when it purchased Longacres Racetrack in Renton for about $82 million. Longacres, built in 1933, was a gem of a track, easily accessible, and well regarded in racing circles. Some 1,800 people worked there at its peak, from veterinarians to breeders to jockeys and stable boys. (At my ten-year high school reunion, it seemed as though everybody who did not work for Boeing worked for Longacres.) But the Alhadeff family, which founded and still owned the track, said it could no longer economically justify the endeavor, and so sold the site to Boeing. The 215-acre tract, once known as "the Jim Nelsen farm," was about to get its third owner.[27]

Instantly, the thoroughbred racing industry in Western Washington appeared in jeopardy, since Boeing made it clear they wanted this land for corporate facilities, including a glitzy new training center for customers who purchased its new 777 jetliner. Boeing relented slightly, however, and let racing continue at the track for one more year and then another.

For the nearby cities, roads and utilities again became issues of concern. "Fred Stewart was in charge of Everett, then Longacres, and wanted to redeem himself in corporate eyes. Boeing at first said it wouldn't pay for anything," said one local official. This time Renton got $10 million in mitigation payments from Boeing for Longacres, and Tukwila got another $2.5 million. Most of the money was intended for transportation improvements. "Everett screwed them over [on the 777 plant addition; see below] and we said, 'OK, what do you need?'" Covington said. "We tried to say, 'What do we both need?'" Some racing interests would not give up, however, and sued the company and the city of Renton to stop destruction of the track facilities and construction of Boeing's new buildings.

As with Sanford Webb, Boeing was forced to joust with yet another gray knight. This time it was Chris Clifford, a restaurant owner and, like Webb, a frequent, unsuccessful candidate for local office. Clifford linked up with a pro-racing citizens' group, and they challenged every move Boeing made at Longacres, from razing the old buildings on the site (Clifford said various species of raptors had taken up residence in the buildings) to charging that the city had issued permits prematurely. Some members of the citizens' group called for turning the site into a horse-racing memorial. Boeing won each step, before the city and before the courts. Clifford later said he was not anti-Boeing, he just thought they should have to play by the rules. In the end, it was difficult to see what difference it made, or where Boeing had stepped out of bounds. In Clifford's one victory, a judge ruled that Renton had issued a permit to Boeing prematurely. But she declined to make the city or the company do anything as a result.

Boeing officials said the delays, however, were maddening. "The problem is anyone with $75 and Roger Leeds's phone number [Leeds is a prominent local environmental attorney] can stop your project in its tracks," grumbled one executive. The delays and legal costs also were expensive, though company officials declined to put an exact price on the adventure. "No average company could have gone through that and survived," Coffey later said of the Longacres steeplechase.

Even more than money, however, Boeing officials were concerned with time. "Money they got; time they don't," said one former Boeing construction manager. Though they were never clear on what the delay really cost them, Boeing officials were firm in their unhappiness. The company was pitching sales for its new 777 based in part on providing high-tech pilot training at Longacres; any delay lessened the allure of that pitch.

And still, Boeing's dance with Renton was not complete. The company also sought to extend the Renton runway apron at the edge of Lake Washington. Aircraft leaving the Renton assembly line have to do a U-turn out the door on their way to the Renton Municipal Airport runway. Extending the apron would have made that easier, and, city officials hoped, would allow the company to move production of the 767 (Boeing's third largest jet after the 747 and the 777) from Everett to Renton. It looked like a win-win bargain for city and company; Renton would expedite the permits and Boeing would contribute money to help with dredging the mouth of the Cedar River. "We were on the same side of the issue. It was a real eye-opener for them. It helped Boeing understand how government works," Covington said.

Most of the time, government does not flow like a river. The Cedar River rolls out of the Cascade Mountains. Most of its upper reaches are encased in a City of Seattle watershed, its progress impeded only by the Landsburg Dam. The dam is not big enough to hold back much water when rain and snowmelt contribute to serious flooding, which happens at least once every decade. That problem is exacerbated by the build-up of silt deposits at the mouth of the river in the shallows of Lake Washington. So from time to time, the City of Renton endeavors to dredge the mouth of the Cedar.

For most of the city's history, that meant hiring heavy equipment big enough to do the job. Tougher environmental laws have made the process more difficult. Renton tried to start another round of dredging in 1987. "Everybody I talked to thought it was a great idea," Renton mayor Clymer said. Money for the dredging was appropriated by the legislature but was vetoed by Governor Gardner, and the project languished.

The city said the flood that followed cost it $4 million, and cost Boeing considerably more in damaged equipment at the Renton plant. The company agreed to contribute to the dredging project, with the benefit of being able to use the spoils to extend its runway apron into Lake Washington. That would allow the company to build widebody jets in Renton. Keeping or bringing more jobs to Renton would boost city receipts via the head tax.

Again, geography played a role. An area with fewer wetlands would not have been as affected by the federal government's no-net-loss-of-wetlands policy. Government played its part, too: the various permits for the dredging, especially those from the U.S. Army Corps of Engineers, had to be pursued consecutively and not concurrently, which strung out the project for two more years.

By 1993, everything seemed ready to go, when the Muckleshoot Indian Tribe stepped in and said no. Using the dredge spoils to extend Boeing's apron could harm fish habitat, the tribe argued, and the two sides could not work out a deal. Unofficially, sources close to the negotiation said, the tribe wanted a lot more money than Boeing was willing to spend. The city eventually did dredge the river mouth, with the spoils hauled away and dumped in Puget Sound. The demise of the plan meant that Boeing did not fund construction of a fish-spawning channel in the Cedar.

Renton officials were disappointed, although not with Boeing. "They're very good neighbors to us," Mayor Clymer said of Boeing, which still contributed the money it had promised for the city's dredging operation, despite the setback on the apron. Of course, the company also stood to benefit from the reduced threat of flooding.

EVERETT

Boeing came to Everett because it ran out of room everywhere else. The Seattle and Renton plants were busy and full, nor was there much room to expand at either site. Building the world's largest jetliner—the 747—would require the world's largest building.

Everett incorporated in 1893. Like a lot of places in Western Washington, it started out and long remained a mill town. Into the 1980s, you could not drive by on Interstate 5 without catching the scent of lumber and sawdust and pulp. Eventually it became an aerospace town as well. As with a lot of things in this story, much of Boeing's involvement with Everett started by chance. Boeing launched the 747 program in part because Lockheed won the federal contract to build the C-5A military transport (in part because the company promised to put final assembly in the home district of the U.S. Senate Armed Services Committee chairman).[28] With rising demand for airliners and some plans for a big jet on the boards, and Pan Am founder Juan Trippe egging on Boeing chairman Bill Allen, the 747 seemed a worthwhile consolation prize.

But there was no obvious reason to build the 747 anywhere near Seattle, especially in light of what had just happened with the C-5A.

> Politics suggested California as the most obvious site. It had the strongest aerospace industry and thus the most powerful aerospace lobby. A massive Boeing plant in the region would woo some of the local politicians away from Douglas, then Boeing's major competitor.[29]

Internally, Boeing was split on the issue. Many in the company felt as though they had been jobbed by the government on both the C-5A and the TFX fighter, and a California plant might help prevent a similar outcome in the future.[30] Others at headquarters thought the insulated local culture had made the company stronger.[31] And despite Washington's relatively small population, in U.S. Senators Warren Magnuson and Henry Jackson Boeing also had two heavy hitters in the other Washington already on its side.

Everett had an airport, Paine Field, with a 10,000-foot runway, and that put it on Boeing's short list for 747 plant sites in the mid-1960s. But the city started out no higher than fifth on Boeing's list, behind candidates including San Diego; Denver; Moses Lake, Washington; Cleveland; and Livermore, California. San Francisco and Los Angeles also were considered. Boeing even took an option on land in Walnut Creek near Oakland, recognizing both California's political clout and the site's proximity to many Boeing subcontractors. That plan never took flight.

It quickly became apparent, however, that placing the plant near Oakland instead of in the Puget Sound region would severely disrupt the 747 project. The impact would be especially hard on personnel. People involved in development would have to move, many would refuse, and replacements would have to be hired. This would slow down development.[32]

Miss Congeniality was a site near McChord Air Force Base in Pierce County, south of Seattle, but the holders of two parcels within the site refused to sell. Boeing took an option on land in Everett in June 1966, and the city agreed to add a freeway junction to ease traffic to the site.[33] So Boeing went to Everett,[34] and rapidly became the area's largest employer. (By a lot, in fact; in 1992, Snohomish County figures showed Boeing with 24,174 employees; the Edmonds School District, in second place, had 2,807.)[35] It was, as Clive Irving noted, a "sweetheart deal," with the city selling Boeing the land and contributing a freeway interchange to provide better access to it.[36]

Everett became a permitting benchmark and the stuff of company legend. Boeing, struggling to stay alive, built the Everett facility virtually as it was building the first 747s. Permits were easy then, and the facility went up without a hitch. (The experience had further repercussions for Boeing's construction projects. During the company's darkest days in 1969–71, some of its contractors did not push for rapid payment, helping to keep their customer afloat. An ex-facilities manager later said that even into the 1990s, Boeing executives let bids go to those contractors even when they were not the low bidders on some projects, apparently out of gratitude for their help on the Everett plant.)

The Everett expansion was not destined to be like the initial project, however. Everett was to slide from glory to gory as the company and the city battled over who should pay for what. In the 1980s, Boeing wrestled with a number of concepts while looking to expand its product line. A high-mileage, mid-size jet, the 7J7, was scrapped after several years of research when fuel costs moderated later in the decade. Eventually, the company settled on the 777, the world's largest twinjet, a widebody that would signal enormous change in how Boeing built its jetliners. The product and all its parts would be designed in teams, so that mechanics and machinists and flight attendants and pilots could tell engineers what would work and what would not. It also was designed completely on computer, and built without a mockup.

But the revolutionary jet would require more space for its construction. Renton was busy with 737s and 757s, and Everett was full with 747s and 767s. Boeing had room to grow at Everett and so, in March 1990, chose to expand what already was the world's largest building by another 5.6 million square feet, at a cost of $1.7 billion.

Boeing predicted that its Everett expansion would bring in 9,500 employees, two-thirds of whom would buy homes near the plant. And yet the psalm among employees, including managers, is that there is never any point in moving, because you are going to get transferred again anyway. One 777 manager, despite a couple of years on the project, continued to live two counties south in Bonney Lake. But Boeing appeared to play it safe in impact statements filed with the city, suggesting a need for as many as 7,666 new housing units, and 6,662 new school desks for the new employees' dependents. Total Everett Boeing employment was to rise from 24,000 in 1991 to 33,500 in 1994.[37] Boeing's plans included high-rise office towers as well as expanded manufacturing capacity at its Paine Field site.

For Everett, this was decidedly a mixed blessing (and another example of the Paradox of Growth). Boeing's plans seemed destined to put strains on the city's and county's stock of housing, roads, and schools. Stepping into the middle of this was Pete Kinch, newly installed as mayor in 1989 after more than a decade on the city council. Kinch said the biggest challenge was meeting the requirements of the Growth Management Act, which said local governments had to plan for important public needs— such as schools and roads and housing. "We were plowing new ground," Kinch recalled. For Boeing, he said, "Obviously, time was money." But hiring more people to expedite the largest construction project the city had ever seen was in itself problematic. "As a political leader you're graded on not expanding the city work force, so you get criticized if you add more people."

Kinch said the company was "very professional" in its dealings with the city. Part of the problem, he said, was that the project was so big that Boeing parceled out the environmental studies to different consultants, and city officials had to make all those pieces fit. Boeing told the city it cost them $1 million for each day of delay. "Boeing literally had the bulldozers and the earth-moving equipment on site and ready to go, and the planners were still fiddling with the EIS," Kinch said. He said he saved some time by sending city planners to Boeing consultants to "sit down and get it to work out. Don't keep them coming back and forth every day." The city of Everett originally asked for more than $50 million in transportation improvements and $2 million for low-income housing assistance, presumably because the new Boeing workers would displace some low-income residents.

From the outset, other challenges to Boeing's plans started taking off like aircraft before Thanksgiving. The Snohomish County Alliance to End Homelessness decided Boeing should pay $10 million to $20 million to offset the need for 2,700 low-income housing units that would be generated because of the plant expansion. That was about ten times more than the city of Everett was requiring of the company (which could raise the question of why the company should pay anything at all). An attorney for the alliance said they did not want to delay the project, but rather to force the city to make Boeing pay more.[38] The local transit authority, another nearby city, and something called Citizens for Responsible Development also asked for more money, to all of which the Everett City Council said no. Concerns ranged from wetlands mitigation to noise reduction.

The Snohomish County Council originally asked for $25.6 million in impact fees, including $9.2 million for roads and $8.1 million for housing. The county also thought Boeing should pay $5 million to help the county acquire park land, $2.85 million for "indirect surface water impacts," and $1 million for "law and justice funding." The council started and then dropped an appeal of the project, after snatching $10.4 million of the original $50 million for transportation improvements.[39]

After Boeing project managers negotiated the Everett expansion mitigation plan, corporate leaders reviewed it and were unhappy. Privately, some Boeing executives said the company had waited too long to decide to build the 777, thereby not leaving themselves with any time to work out a deal with Everett (a point that probably would be disputed by some Boeing marketeers). Publicly, however, company officials were livid at the prospect of what they saw as paying millions of dollars to bring more jobs to a community.

Little more than a month later, Shrontz made his speech. He noted that it would have been 30 to 40 percent cheaper to build the plant in Wichita or Huntsville, Alabama, the sites of Boeing's other large plants. A Snohomish County Councilman replied that "Improvements must be made in proportion to size of development."[40] He must not have known about the story a few pages away, in which a Denver group was offering twenty-three acres of land and $80 million in construction funds if only Boeing would build something at the city's new airport.[41]

Mayor Kinch quickly felt the heat:

> We got beat to a pulp on that. I understood what Boeing was doing and why, but I never really appreciated the fact that we were made an example. We were caught between a rock and a hard place. We had to mitigate the project; that was state law and we had to apply it. They ended up using that example in the press and the legislature and Everett became the greedy, grubby little city that should be glad to have that plant there.... If you're going to apply the law in the mitigation process, I think it was done about as fair as anybody's done it.

Kinch said he understood that Boeing had to send a signal to others, however. "Boeing is in a number of communities in the state and they didn't want the state legislature getting big dollar signs in their eyes and asking for a bunch of money."

Kinch also was aware that Boeing's expansion had other locations scrambling to get the aerospace giant to relocate. "There were cities all over the country that were begging them to come there. A $1.5 billion expansion! Cities and states would kill for that. Cities were offering them free land. It was not a comfortable thing to have to do in a competitive environment. The one thing we could do for them was to be a player, to be efficient in the process." Eighteen months to process the EIS, he said, was "extremely fast for something of that magnitude."

Boeing officials like to point out that it took eighteen months to *build* the original 747 building—from applying for the permits to unlocking the front door—and that the same permits would take all of a month to get in Wichita.[42] "The millions of dollars spent on consultant fees for various environmental reviews, the cost of two and a half years of staff time to manage the process, and $50 million in mitigation fees significantly impact the cost of doing business and, therefore, the cost of our product in a highly competitive global marketplace," Boeing senior vice-president Doug Beighle said in a speech about the subject. Nonetheless, Everett Boeing general manager Ed Renouard later said the project was completed on schedule and within budget.[43]

The expansion helped produce one interesting side effect: Kinch opposed resuming commercial service at Paine Field, in part because if the airport got too busy, Boeing might leave. "I felt it was very important that we don't shoot ourselves in the foot," he said. Boeing made no public pronounce-ments on the issue, other than to urge the region to keep up with its airport needs.

Kinch was unelected for his troubles, but others agreed that the system had squeezed the city. John Thoresen, president of the Snohomish County Economic Development Council, characterized the Growth Management Act as "saying nothing gets built unless the infrastructure is in place. The problem with the GMA was there were no funds to pay for everything. And here's the Boeing Company saying 'We want to add 10,000 people.' What's that going to do to traffic and housing and schools? This community had just looked at what the Navy was going to do [the U.S. Navy was concur-rently building a homeport for an aircraft carrier group at Everett]. We had two of the largest development projects in the country going on at the same time."

Everett found itself amid the Paradox of Growth. The GMA's require-ments, in one sense, were an understandable reaction to years of growth that had long since outstripped the local infrastructure's ability to handle it. Requiring such infrastructure to keep pace with growth is not even nec-essarily antigrowth; lack of roads, housing, and public facilities would eventually discourage growth as surely as high taxes and impact fees. The legislature might be faulted for not providing funds to pay for the GMA, but there again, raising taxes would discourage growth as capably as bad planning would.

Thoresen pointed out what Renton's Covington also knew: Washington cities make money from sales tax, and have a difficult time financing im-provements that do not generate tax revenues. "It's more important for the city to get Costco [than] it is from a financial standpoint to get XYZ Man-ufacturing," he said. "Everett added $1 million from a single Costco store. Until we get the tax structure changed, that's what's going to happen."

But Thoresen also blamed local officials for their approach to the prob-lem. "At the time, the political climate was much different than it is today," he said in 1996. "There was, in some of the political leadership, probably an us-against-them kind of mentality." Business was viewed as not paying its fair share of the benefits it was reaping. In the aftermath of Shrontz's warn-ing, however, things changed. "We had some zealous no-growth people on the city council in the late 1980s, and they're gone," Thoresen said.

Something else changed: the aerospace market. Everett and Snohomish

County were saved by the bell as much as by their own efforts. As the aerospace business cycle took a sharp turn south, Boeing's expected demands on Everett's infrastructure failed to materialize. The 777 addition was completed in Everett, but the predicted stream of workers did not arrive until much later. Although 6,500 workers were transferred to Everett as 777 production began to gear up, total Everett employment leveled off at about 27,000. And although the region's economic expansion continued (albeit at about 1 percent a year), Boeing's downsizing eased the pressures of growth—and once again temporarily saved the area from having to confront the Paradox. Boeing eventually neared its employment projections as production levels soared in response to demand in 1997 and 1998, resuming strains on housing and transportation. The broader patterns of what was driving this—the conflict between managing growth and economic development, and the recurring nature of that conflict—seemed lost on most observers.

But Boeing kept hammering for regulatory reform, and Everett and Snohomish County scrambled to get back in the company's good graces. Boeing, its expansion plans scaled back, asked for a delay on signing checks for $15 million of the money it had agreed to pay Everett. Mayor Kinch said he would seek assurances from the company that future Boeing jets would be developed and built in Everett.[44]

Snohomish County executive Bob Drewel gathered the usual suspects—business and government leaders, including Jim Johnson, now Everett Boeing general manager—"and created an economic development plan for Snohomish County so this wouldn't happen again," said Thoresen. "I think they recognized that they needed to step up and do a better job ... on educating the public on wealth creation."

The city and the county used a state grant to try to integrate the Growth Management Act and the State Environmental Protection Act, so as to smooth the permitting process for a parcel adjacent to Paine Field, and made a prominent pronouncement that the land was available for Boeing if it should need it. "This isn't just a plan to help Boeing grow," however, Thoresen said, noting that education was at the top of the agenda and that improvements in permitting and taxes would be enjoyed by all businesses. (Boeing accepted a five-year right of first refusal on the hundred-acre site, but said it had no plans to use it.)[45] Thoresen cautioned against missing the obvious. "They're a major influence," he said of Boeing. "It's not just because they're the Boeing Company, it's because they have almost 30,000 workers in this county."

News in the early 1990s of ongoing layoffs at Boeing certainly underscored the cities' concerns. As usual, Boeing's response was careful and effective. Preserving its image as the good corporate citizen, in late 1993 and early 1994 the company opened reemployment centers in Renton and Everett, offering a variety of training and related resources. "We decided we had to do a better job for our people," Bud Coffey said at the dedication at Renton in December 1993. The facilities were paid for by Boeing, the state, and the federal government; predictably, Boeing was extremely close-mouthed about the centers' rates of success. Students were referred to community colleges for retraining, but could only enroll in the programs where chances were good of moving on to new jobs.

The sum of Boeing's experiences with its host communities is that the cities, burdened by an antiquated tax structure and unfunded state mandates, had nowhere to turn (other than to Boeing itself) when forced to provide the infrastructure to support plant expansion. Furthermore, long-standing concerns about growth had led to creation of a permitting system that appeared elephantine compared to areas with less population density and more room to grow. Boeing officials frequently pointed to rapid permit grants in Tukwila, Pierce County, and Spokane. Urban/industrial Tukwila is virtually built out, effectively making growth a nonissue, and Pierce County and Spokane have comparatively more open land and fewer people than does the King–Snohomish County area.

But perhaps the most frustrating challenges, at least from Boeing's point of view, came not from municipal officials but from the bewildering array of citizens' groups, all of whom were largely concerned with what amount to quality-of-life issues. And these were issues that did not exist until population growth threatened to turn Pugetopia into Pugetropolis. Snohomish County's population, for example, grew 30 percent in the 1980s.[46] That kind of growth, wedged in between the mountains and the Sound, spawned constituencies that a generation before would have been not only beating the drum but also leading the march for economic growth.

At the municipal level, Boeing seems to have got some of what it wanted, at least in the near term. Shrontz's 1991 speech echoed up and down Puget Sound, Boeing public affairs manager Terry Lewis said. "I have a feeling that they've heard our message ever since the Shrontz speech," he said. "They [local officials] understand what we're trying to accomplish. When we walk in the door with a specific problem I think they understand what we want." Still, he was not convinced that any changes would be permanent. "The interesting test is the next time we do something in Everett," Lewis said.

7 / Calling in the Cavalry

After all is said and done, more is generally said than done.
—Mike Fitzgerald, director, Washington State Department
of Trade and Economic Development

Every Seattle-area problem seems to get studied to death.
—Neal R. Peirce

THE CITIES could do only so much to placate the big kid on the block; the basic problem, the Growth Management Act, was a state law and would have to be resolved at the state level. Among the GMA's problems was that portions of it contradicted the existing State Environmental Policy Act (SEPA). For example, in the early 1990s Boeing wanted to redevelop its Duwamish corridor area into a research and development center, eventually employing up to 25,000 people. But whereas GMA encouraged such densities to minimize widespread environmental impact, SEPA discouraged them, also for environmental reasons. "We found that if we increased density in the area, it triggered millions of dollars of mitigation costs for improving highways," said Andy Gay, Boeing facilities vice-president. "The most cost-effective business approach was to cap our employment below historical levels so we would not trigger these costs. So although the GMA policy is to encourage density and promote concurrency, the actual result was to reduce density and avoid concurrency."[1]

Boeing had quite a shopping list of problems by then, including four different sets of conflicting handrail regulations, being asked to subsidize carpools and bus ridership while being asked to pay for more highways, and an appeals process that allowed development projects to be challenged at least six different times. "There are over 4,800 federal, state, county, and

municipal regulators focused on King County and only 3,100 law enforcement officers," Gay lamented.[2]

In 1993, Chairman Shrontz met with Governor Mike Lowry, and Lowry
responded. Faced with an unhappy camper of remarkable size, the governor did what any politician in Washington State who was expecting re-
election would do: he convened a commission. "Back east, they call this
the land of process," Glenn Pascall once said of Washington State. The
Governor's Task Force on Regulatory Reform was classic Washington State
politics: consensual, deliberative, and somewhat cumbersome. The twenty-
one-member commission included representatives from labor, business,
agriculture, state agencies, the legislature, and local government.

At the outset, Lowry told the commission to make the state "a great
place to do business and a great place to live." He also instructed state
agencies to forward proposed changes to rules to the state's Business Assistance Center so they could make them more easily understood.[3] "It's way
more complicated than it should be," Lowry said of the state's regulatory
and permit process.[4]

In an address to the Economic Development Council of King County in
1993, Lowry said his regulatory reform commission would "deal in speci-
fics, not generalities," and said it was among his top priorities. He called for
ending duplicative regulations at the various levels of government, as well
as for the usual collection of better schools, improved infrastructure, and
public-private partnerships. "We need regulatory reform and we will get
that," the governor said.

As the commission formed and began to meet, Boeing continued its
harangue against the state and region. Senior Vice-President Doug Beighle
said the state had an antibusiness environment, including a tax structure
that is not good for business. "We told the economic task force of the
governor that this area is not competitive." Coffey, who had landed a place
on the panel, added that the cost of doing business in Washington was
approaching that of California. "You can live with that if you've got some
certainty," Beighle said. "The environmental process certainly doesn't provide much certainty."

Within Boeing, some company officials even argued that some production or jobs should be moved to Wichita, "just to make a point." The
usual difficulties associated with such a move seemed to preclude it, but,
aided by ongoing layoffs, the discussion revved up the rumor mill to a
steady hum.

Boeing made its case to the panel when the peripatetic Regulatory Reform Commission's road show came to Boeing headquarters in Seattle. President Condit compared the commission's challenge to Boeing's: bringing diverse elements together in close cooperation to achieve a mutual goal. He added that the time it was taking to get permits was slowing down the company's ability to do business. "If you had to order from a restaurant a day and a half before you wanted to eat, that wouldn't be good," he said. "It's not meant as a threat; it's a reality."

Coffey complained that "it doesn't do us any good to get an internal pricing structure that's competitive and still have an external structure that isn't." He said that he thought the commission should "look at the most onerous issues that are causing regulatory problems. Pick two or three things," and work on those. Among those, he cited the appeals process. "You can stop any project today for $75," Coffey said, by simply filing a court challenge. "There ought to be a process where you can say 'This project is a go.'" But he acknowledged the difficulty of steering reform through the legislative labyrinth. "If we go down there by ourselves and say 'we've got problems,'" the legislature won't listen as closely.

"The governor knows he's got to get something on the books," Coffey said, if only for political reasons. By 1994, however, Boeing officials confided that they were not impressed with the Regulatory Reform Commission's lack of progress. "The governor talks a good game," Coffey said. Chairwoman Karen Lane's leadership skills were questioned, and the eight private-sector representatives were outnumbered by a dozen public-sector, union, and environmentalist members. Lane was pragmatic in response. "It took us thirty years to get to this (regulatory) impasse. There's not a magic bullet that will get us out."[5]

The commission made a series of modest proposals that went before the legislature in 1994. They cleared the house and senate, only to be vetoed by a dissatisfied Lowry. By late 1994, Boeing officials were not optimistic about regulatory reform. "You're not going to see it resolved," said Rob Makin, a lobbyist for Boeing in Olympia. "It's over balance of power. Who's got power—the legislative or the administrative branch?" The veto of round one came at the behest of state agencies, he said, not from environmentalists.

It is not clear that any of this was having much impact inside government, however. The state agency most responsible for economic concerns, the Washington State Department of Community, Trade, and Economic Development, produced a report on the growth management question that was nearly devoid of economic content. *Integrating SEPA and GMA: The Promise* was rather reminiscent of an early post-Soviet Russian aviation sales pitch: a forthright recollection of the state's administrative capacity to regulate, without reference to what any of it might mean. The report did note that the 1994 legislature had appropriated funds to provide for SEPA and GMA reconciliation,[6] but gave only a slight nod to developers' concerns about the regulations.

Boeing kept up its full-court press. Andy Gay, the taciturn vice-president for facilities, testified before a legislative committee, making the usual comparisons about doing business then and now, here and there. (Inevitably, comparisons are made to the wicked Wichita of the east, the mere mention of which makes Western Washingtonians shiver.) Gay claimed that to get a construction permit in Washington State, the company had to go through fifty-two agencies and follow fifty-five separate regulations. This led to delays of eighteen to twenty-four months on important projects and impaired "our ability to respond to the marketplace."[7] One member of the panel, State Representative Betty Sue Morris, was from Wichita. "There's very little environment there for them to protect," she said.[8] ("We have a wetland," a Kansas economic development official once told me. "But it's a long way from Wichita.")

Gay noted that Boeing spent $3 million on consulting fees in Everett, had to lease temporary office space there, waited eighteen months for the necessary permits, and ultimately paid the city $47 million.[9] Gay was not alone, however. Also testifying were Paul Roberts, Everett planning and community development director, and labor and social service representatives. The inference—costing Boeing money costs jobs which is bad for all of us—could not have been clearer, even to a legislative committee. Roberts would not take all the blame, however. He put the city's price tag for the Everett project at $150 million, and noted that Everett had joined Boeing to help turn back eight appeals to make Boeing pay more money.[10]

"It probably is a problem," said Environmental Committee chairwoman and state representative Nancy Rust, a frequent Boeing critic who helped push the GMA through. Darlene Madenwald of the Washington Environmental Council was not quite as sure, however. "We will fight very hard not to have the GMA eroded in this legislative session," she said. "The GMA is good and most businesses know it's good."[11] Others disagreed. Seattle attorney J. Tayloe Washburn, chairman of the Seattle Chamber of Commerce's Growth Management Task Force, said local governments faced the prospect of trying to balance twenty-five different statewide planning goals, some of which conflicted with each other. "What we're talking about here is mission impossible," he said.[12]

Whatever the opposition, Boeing had little trouble convincing its allies to enlist in the regulatory reform crusade. In early 1995, the Washington Roundtable, a bully pulpit and research arm for the state's biggest companies, issued a prescription for economic health that dovetailed with Boeing's wish list: improve attitudes about business, measure "economic climate indicators" to guide economic development policy, "invest in human capital," improve infrastructure, protect quality of life, and streamline the regulatory process. That these might be conflicting goals was overlooked or ignored. The point man this time, however, was John Rindlaub, CEO of Seafirst Bank, a Bank of America unit and the state's biggest financial institution.

> Washington's attraction as a place to live and do business is increasingly at risk to national and international competition. We must recognize our competition and develop aggressive strategies for improvement so that our children and grandchildren have economic opportunities. If not they will ultimately pay the price in terms of lost jobs.[13]

Meanwhile, Boeing took the lead on yet another initiative, one that spoke of its general clout in the community. Led by a handful of top business leaders, including Boeing's Beighle, the Seattle-area business community in 1994 convened a forum on economic development efforts. The goal was to rationalize the miasma of programs and get, ultimately, more result for the rupee. In April 1995, after meeting for two days at Boeing's corporate cafeteria, the leadership cabal of what was calling itself "The Funders Group" dismissed the community leaders back to their warrens and called in the press corps.

Beighle told reporters that the group had established broad policy goals and, moreover, had assigned responsibility for them to specific economic development agencies. King County executive Gary Locke and Seattle mayor Norm Rice added their public blessings to the effort. In less than a year each would launch gubernatorial campaigns based in part on their status as pro-business centrists; in Locke's case, that was despite a long-standing voting record as an antibusiness state legislator.

The steering committee included a bank president, a former power company executive and current EDC chairman, and the executive director of the Port of Seattle. Each spoke affirmatively of the effort, and unlike so many economic development conferences of recent years, this one appeared to have a plan and also—if only because the big players such as Boeing were the entities that paid the bills—the clout to make something happen. "We're not looking at reducing our funding," Beighle said. "We're looking at making it more effective."

The objectives included most of Boeing's wish list—transit, better schools, improving the business climate. Of course they were not alone in calling for such things, and particularly in the area of business climate, managers from much smaller businesses who had been brought into the program were in complete support. But some issues dear to small businesses, such as tax reform, fell off the Funders Group list. There was no broad consensus around the issue, and it was not one cited by Boeing executives as a top priority.

In less than a year, the Funders Group had refined its targets to five broad areas: greater business-government cooperation, increasing real average wages, job retention, job creation, and maintaining economic vitality and quality of life. "The Puget Sound region is our home and we're committed to building a strong economy that benefits everyone," Beighle said at the press conference.

Boeing's pronouncements on the regulatory issue always were careful. When Condit spoke to a statewide gathering of municipal officials in September 1995, he underlined the impact of regulations not on Boeing, but on small firms, thousands of which "make decisions about where to locate every year." He also said Boeing was not about to pack up and go. "We have a tremendous investment in the Puget Sound area," Condit said after the speech. "You don't pick up and move big factories in a hurry. But we're also going to be making future decisions about where to make things."

Governor Lowry, increasingly hamstrung by allegations of sexual harassment by a former press aide, said he remained intent on regulatory reform. It appeared as though the big piece of the legislation, reconciling SEPA and GMA, probably would not come before the 1995 session. But Lowry said it had to be done. "We've got to have an integrated policy with land, air, water, and transportation included," he said. "We're making good progress. Let's not miss some of the good things going on."

Following Republican victories in the 1994 state elections, in 1995 the legislature passed Substitute House Bill 1724, integrating the Growth Management Act and the State Environmental Policy Act. The Association of

Washington Businesses supported the measure, which meant that, at a minimum, Boeing did not disapprove of it. It was part of a broad package of bills aimed at reforming the regulatory process that year. The package gave local governments more leeway on meeting GMA requirements and attempted to rein in the authority of several regulatory agencies. Boeing officials never did say much about it; it is not hard to imagine that politically, they did not want anybody to relax. The legislature followed that up in 1996 by partially leashing the three growth management hearings boards, which critics said had gone from reviewing policy decisions to making them.[14]

In the meantime, the aerospace cycle turned up as sharply as it had fallen. Boeing began booking orders again, and the economy's slow growth began to get robust as the national economy recovered as well. Pascall said Boeing's virtual acquisition of McDonnell Douglas might mean "a steady state Boeing," with fewer employment swings.[15] It seemed, for the moment, that everything was solved. In reality, however, very little had been.

8 / Soft Landing

We are more in danger of locking ourselves out than pushing ourselves in. It's very difficult to focus this metropolitan area on anything.

—James Ellis, Seattle attorney and civic activist

IT WOULD BE TOO EASY to conclude that Boeing, in apparently getting what it wanted, exercised real power, even if it took several years to accomplish. Until the company undertakes another major plant expansion, or pursues some other large-scale, immediate policy objective, we will not know whether those gains were of any lasting value. But using the tools unsheathed in the prologue, we may draw some conclusions about what the Battle of Seattle says about community power.

Although class-based politics long were a feature of Seattle-area governments, the high wages paid by Boeing—and the strength of its unions—largely removed class as an issue for the company, with the possible exception of calls for more support for low-income housing. At a critical juncture, when Boeing sought to navigate the permitting process in Everett, the union saw its interests as being clearly in line with those of the company. No theory of false consciousness is needed to explain that.

As elite theorists predicted, the Seattle area has a growth coalition, which rallied to Boeing's cause as soon as the banner was raised. But it was a different set of elites who generated growth management efforts in the first place. Elites were the key players in the contest, but often in opposition to each other. And, as pluralists would surely surmise, Boeing's plans generated rather widespread competition among myriad groups. In fact, the model that emerges of the state's political experience as a whole would appear to be broadly pluralist, with a significant number of groups competing for political outcomes. The fact that some groups did better than others does not render the competition any less meaningful (despite the usual leftist rejoinder to any evidence of pluralism: "if there was competition, it was not meaningful"). Competition implies outcomes that often are uneven.

Boeing had mixed results at agenda control, however. Although it was able to stand off Seattle when it came to annexation, its supposed dominance of the state legislature largely failed when it came to growth management. The reforms it sought, to ameliorate what it saw as the flaws in growth management, were not insignificant, but came only at great cost. Nor is it likely that Boeing, ultimately, will have circumvented the Paradox of Growth.

Ironically, if Boeing were to realize all its goals with regard to government, it might ultimately make things worse. Just as existing businesses and citizens cannot be excluded from sharing in the costs of growth management, neither can incoming firms and people be excluded from the benefits of public policy. If the company gained a sterling regulatory climate, adequate infrastructure, and a high quality of life, more businesses would be tempted to move here, and people would surely follow. Eventually, the challenges of growth would begin anew.

Business itself, including Boeing, demonstrated some power in achieving its goals, but only at considerable expense and with considerable skill. A less subtle approach could easily have generated more antigrowth backlash and galvanized opposition to the company's plans. More worthy opponents than Chris Clifford and Sandy Webb might have sprung into the fray. Boeing's victory was partial at best—it still spent millions of dollars in mitigation expenses and related costs—and was by no means a foregone conclusion.

As predicted by pluralist theory, we saw competition between numerous groups. As predicted by elite theory, the competition was, at times, raggedly uneven. Not least among the competitors, however, was government itself. Government's responses, in the face of the structural challenge of the Paradox of Growth, seem to have left no one completely satisfied. Whether through legislative action or bureaucratic fiat, state and local governments demonstrated an independence that would not have been predicted by much of existing theory. These governments attempted to respond affimatively to a wide range of citizen concerns. It is clear, however, at least at the executive and legislative levels, that government ultimately recognized its "unitary interest" in fostering economic prosperity. Why? Because without a sufficient employment and revenue base, government can do very little for anyone. This conclusion firmly supports Sell's First Law, *The decision will be made in the direction of the greatest value. Usually that's money.*

What occurred also supported the Second Law: *Politics is economic competition carried on by other means.* Government became the arena for competition between groups aided and abraded by growth, and by interests ultimately concerned with the disposition of wealth generated by a major industry—aerospace.

Also vindicated is the Third Law, *Economic interests will be politically dominant only to the extent that they are economically dominant.* The Boeing of the 1920s through the 1970s did not face the regional challenges shouldered by the Boeing of the 1980s and 1990s. Its declining influence mirrors the rise of interests whose well-being ostensibly does not depend on the fortunes of the aerospace market. In a broader sense, it is shortsighted to divorce Boeing's success from the region's. If Boeing had never come to Seattle, things would be very different, no doubt involving substantial tradeoffs in terms of jobs, revenue base, and cultural amenities. That something would have taken Boeing's place is uncertain if not doubtful. But in an immediate sense, many citizens simply do not see Boeing intersecting with their lives with any meaningful regularity. As a consequence, Boeing's needs and wants seemed no more important than those of any other large firm, and why, these people asked, should we roll over for them? They didn't.

The Fifth Law, *All life is politics,* was demonstrated by the extent to which Boeing succeeded through building enduring relationships with policymakers at all levels. Those relationships were broad, in terms of community initiatives, and narrow, in terms of contacts built up by lobbyists and executives with state and local officials. Actors who fail to recognize the importance of this will tend to experience problems. Boeing's structurally powerful position in no way guaranteed it victory; its attention to personal and public detail made success more likely.[1]

Structural factors ultimately underlay a lot of what happened. Boeing itself faced structural obstacles in terms of heightened competition from Airbus, a situation that company officials said drove them to seek better outcomes in dealings with government. But this is not an argument for structuralism—the idea that outside events heavily influence the workings of politics—as much as it is an argument for the ecological approach. So many factors came into play that to ignore any of them would have been to lose important pieces of the mosaic of community power. By using the whole tool kit, we are able to adequately describe what happened and why, and to predict what will happen down the runway.

The other wing of this story is that given the widespread assumptions both about Boeing and about the dominance of big business in general, the kind of obstacles Boeing faced while *trying to create jobs* should not have occurred. But the demands of the Paradox of Growth meant that a well-regarded company, a company that by skill and habit had knitted itself into the economic and social fabric of the region, found itself at odds with governments that one would expect to be giddy over the prospect of plant expansion and added employment.

One might as easily conclude that Northwest people are just different, and it would be wrong to write off the socialization aspects of living here. Environmental and process expectations here are different, but not enough to produce such disputes between Boeing and the region, especially at a time when other states and communities were selling their souls to get factories.

The key ingredient was the presence of the Paradox. The consequences of more growth offered mixed benefits to many people whose livelihoods were not directly tied up in aerospace: more traffic, less open space, higher housing prices (of benefit only to those who plan to sell their houses and move someplace cheaper). It also posed distinct challenges to the governments faced with accommodating that growth. Washington State's peculiar tax structure only intensified that problem.

Boeing's persistence in wading through those problems is due in part to its enormous capital investment in the region, and to its continuing need for skilled workers. A less adroit company might not have overcome the hurdles it faced, and might have opted instead to look seriously at relocation. But Boeing had carefully husbanded its political and financial resources, allowing it to get through an arcane and lengthy process.

In part, at least, it had to. Relocation was a far less viable option than the company will ever admit to publicly. Realistically, few people from Seattle would ever move to Wichita. (As a reporter, for example, I could be sure to get a rise out of any of my public relations counterparts simply by beginning the conversation: "So, I hear they're sending you to Wichita.")

Although many businesses, including developers, tended to approve of the 1995 reform legislation,[2] Boeing officials did not say much. Of course, from a leverage standpoint, one would not expect them to. As Shrontz prepared to retire as chairman and CEO, he said progress had been made on the regulatory front. "I think there's a greater awareness of the problem," he said in June 1996. "I think we clearly have a long way to go. We don't want to defile the environment. We live here. But we object to the bureaucratic way in which some things are handled. I hope that the next governor considers that unfinished business."

But the 1995 legislation did little to address the Paradox of Growth, and may in fact have worsened it. Although Governor Lowry vetoed a partial roll-back of a 1993 increase in the B&O tax (a roll-back that Boeing favored), he let pass a sales tax exemption on new machinery and equipment (which Boeing also supported). The measure was soon celebrated for helping to bring an Intel chip plant near Tacoma, but privately and not so privately, city officials around the Sound began to lament the bite that the tax break was putting on their budgets. The Paradox of Growth will not go away of its own accord; luring new employers without a plan to accommodate costs of the growth they bring with them will only make things worse down the road.

This does not mean nothing can be done. Lowry needed to take charge on regulatory reform; leaving it up to a commission that was inclusive but inefficient left too many of the participants dissatisfied. But Lowry came from Congress, not the state legislature. While he was better than his predecessor, Booth Gardner, at working the Marble Zoo, he was by no means dynamic. Coffey, who had worked hard to convince business to support Lowry in 1992 over the doctrinaire Republican candidate, was particularly disappointed, associates said.

Reconciling the tax-and-growth issue with businesses' needs will take far more initiative and compromise than has been seen in Washington State for some time. Income tax proposals, which in theory would give cities a chance at capturing some revenue from high-paying manufacturing jobs, have been soundly defeated multiple times. (Heaven knows we sure don't want any state tax we'd be able to deduct from our federal income tax, now do we.) Raising other taxes remains politically unpopular, while simply moving spending toward infrastructure needs would steal from other legitimate programs.

Other growth issues, such as controlling urban sprawl, appear similarly intractable. Fundamentally, it appears, public policy makers at both the state and local levels have done nothing to address the issues that raised concerns about growth. The state's two highest growth peaks, in the late

1960s and in the late 1980s, were blunted only by Boeing recessions. As Boeing fortunes soared again in the mid-1990s, I asked a number of people who had previously dealt with the issue if growth-driven problems would start to reappear. Most said they did not think so, but as of 1998 housing prices were soaring again, traffic was worse, pollution was no better, and neither the state nor the cities had any new mechanisms for responding to such concerns. The housing affordability issue in particular appeared to be aggravated by the GMA and the many regulations that still conflict with it, as development consultant Randy Blair pointed out in 1996:

> The harsh reality is that residential subdivisions will have difficulty achieving GMA-mandated densities because of outdated development standards and the public review process required by state subdivision law and local regulations.... Putting six dwelling units on an acre means creating residential lots that are between 40 and 45 feet wide, once provisions for streets, sensitive areas, and storm-water management facilities are made. But many municipalities still have zoning codes requiring corner lots to be 55 to 65 feet wide, and interior lots 50 feet wide.... Designers, builders and owners are as frustrated as city and county staff, since the review procedure causes delays, forces changes to plans, and increases uncertainty. The resulting cost increases are ultimately passed along to homeowners, and contribute to rising home prices in the region.[3]

Furthermore, Blair said, the GMA's goals of increased housing density in developed areas had their own bridges to cross. "While this is a nice concept, the rub is that none of us want higher-density housing in our neighborhoods."[4] Pascall argued that the GMA's push for more cities and fewer unincorporated areas may further exacerbate the problem, weakening counties' ability to deal with growth while adding to the 140-some different government entities all trying to manage growth in the Puget Sound region.[5]

The prospects for serious discussions about managing growth are not all that good. In 1995, Dan Evans lamented the hard-line politics of the current age, which seem to prevent the kind of compromise that might actually resolve the dilemma of growth. "Today everybody wants to play the scorched-earth policy," he said. "Everybody wants to win everything and beat everybody. Too often nobody wins anything." Evans particularly criticized environmental groups. He recalled a 1969 gathering at which five environmental legislative proposals were crafted and pushed through in a thirty-two-day special legislative session. "It was a time of cooperation on issues where everybody won something," he said. That spirit is gone now, he said. "They get arrogant. They get to the point where they think their strength doesn't require compromise anymore. You get too popular and you get arrogant." Evans said regulations, not the laws behind them, may be a big part of the problem. "Regulations can change the intent of the law," he said. "It's the regulatory side of government, frankly, that I think has gotten out of hand. The people who are elected to office are sort of outside the [iron] triangle."

It is, in a sense, the curse of wealth. Mammoth gains in productivity have meant, in part, fewer people making more goods. The wealth thus created generates externalities (as demonstrated above), which leads to more government in an attempt to ameliorate those externalities. Once established, active government takes on a life of its own,[6] prompting, for example, Nobel Prize–winning economist Douglass North to note that "About half the resources in our society are going to people who are not producing anything. They grease the wheels in our economy."[7]

And also slow the wheels down. North argues that government's role should be to reduce transaction costs, not to add to them. "If these costs rise more rapidly than gains in technology, you're in real trouble," he said. "The real dilemma is attempting to understand how society can provide a structure that will encourage human beings to be creative and productive." But "political markets," unfortunately, "are inherently less susceptible to improvements than are economic markets," North said.[8]

In many ways, it took an outfit as big as Boeing to move the political market to try to really address the Paradox of Growth. Boeing is indeed powerful, because of both its size and its assembled skill. It does not dominate the state to the extent that many assume, perhaps, but no other organization can move the public debate as much as Boeing can.

The company's leverage against local and state governments is likely to increase in the next several years. In 1996, Boeing acquired the bulk of Rockwell International's space and defense business, then late in the year announced it was buying long-time rival McDonnell Douglas. The move will allow Boeing to play one plant location off against another, as the California sites it has acquired are much more credible alternatives for relocation than either Wichita or Huntsville. Boeing executives would no doubt deny using such a tactic, even as they trumpet the need for maximum productive efficiency. But you do not have to play a good card if everyone knows you have it. Boeing may not listen seriously to pitches from Atlanta, Denver, and Orlando, but it certainly uses them to gain leverage in Washington State.

Boeing officials have already said that when they get around to building an extra-large, superjumbo jetliner, they may have to look elsewhere as much because of space requirements as because of business climate concerns.[9] Soon after the McDonnell Douglas merger, Condit traveled to Los Angeles to paint a picture of Boeing as a firm with California roots.[10]

The specter of cities and states in competition for business is not a new one, but as the 1990s drew to a close it seemed to be growing. States and localities spent millions of dollars luring factories to the point where many observers questioned whether these investments would ever pay off.[11] Alabama, for example, spent $12 million—$350,000 per job—to get a steel mill to move to Decatur.[12] Conversely, New York City, without a retention strategy and with high taxes, lost 700,000 jobs from 1958 to 1991, even as public sector employment mushroomed.[13] Meanwhile, by the 1980s, two dozen cities and states had opened offices in California. Their mission was to recruit firms there to relocate; their pitch was "Come with us and avoid the high taxes and excessive regulation."[14] Perhaps it was an apocryphal tale, and I could never get it confirmed, but the rumor was that Atlanta had an operative permanently camped in Seattle, whose sole job was to get Boeing to relocate.

Stanley L. Elkin suggests a national reward/penalty system to ease the pressure on cities to compete,[15] but one must wonder whether that would, in the end, simply encourage factory migration outside the United States. A number of social scientists and policy wonks have advocated paying business to surrender some of its privileges—basically so it will not move or lay off large numbers of people.[16] But the notion that the public has some inherent claim on private wealth is uncertain at best and perilous at worse. It underscores a fundamental and widespread misunderstanding about the creation of wealth. The dynamic efficiency of private enterprise is often just better at creating wealth than is public enterprise. Public enterprise's understandable and natural concern with process, consensus, and different modes of equity tends to produce its own set of externalities, such as shackling creativity and encouraging inefficiency. Could the Seattle City Council in its finest hours have built an airplane, let alone an aerospace giant? Aircraft would still be made out of spruce.

There is a case to be made for public management of private resources: by no means do public managers have an exclusive franchise on ineptitude—witness MIT's "Made in America" study, which concluded that most U.S. business managers are relatively myopic.[17] Robert Reich, in his somewhat uneven book *The Next American Frontier*, reached largely the same conclusion: the biggest problem with American business since World War II has been, in fact, American business.[18] And America has no more government involvement in the economy than most of the rest of the developed world, and usually much less.

This leads Charles Lindblom to conclude that polyarchal (democratic) control of decisions about investment, plant location, and work force will not cost more than private control, because business does not know what it is doing.[19] And government does? To do this, you have to pick winners among industries and firms, a task the nation's financial and investment analysts—people who spend lifetimes studying these firms and industries—rarely do well. To date, only the much maligned market has had any success at picking winners; it is one thing markets are actually good at.[20] Moreover, as Moynihan noted, if you try to hold business to normative standards—the way things ought to be, as opposed to how they are—you will politicize it, and this has costs. Not the least of these is beginning to remove business as a check on the state, an independent source of wealth and power to keep government honest. "I would say that the market has a lot more to do with the perpetuation of a democratic and libertarian society than you might think," Moynihan said.[21]

DeLeon notes how the real estate collapse of the mid-1980s affected San Francisco, and rightly calls into question the investment choices of the nation as a whole.[22] But the real estate market eventually recovered, bad decisions notwithstanding. None of capitalism's many off-key tunes has yet become its funeral march. The system, despite its flaws, is remarkably resilient.

Moreover, public managers can hide behind policy debates a lot longer than private managers can; a bad business manager usually does not last very long. The market is unforgiving. When public managers do face accountability, they tend to shift risk away from themselves, which can lead to worse policy outcomes. But for the most part, as Leone says, "public managers tend to be held accountable almost exclusively to process and rarely to outcome."[23] Private managers must be free to take risks, whereas public managers are schooled to avoid them. We have no reason to expect that public managers will be any better at managing business than private ones are, and every reason to expect that they will not. In Alaska, for example, the state's oil wealth allowed it to invest millions of dollars in diversification efforts, including such ventures as barley farming, a dairy industry, and dog-powered washing machines.[24]

> Unfortunately, government revenues are not systematically allocated to their highest valued public use by well-informed and public-spirited political decision-makers. The allocation of tax revenues occurs primarily in response to political pressures brought to bear by organized interest groups, each with a dominant interest in a particular government program.[25]

But the stable and predictable society that allowed Boeing the freedom to grow into a successful firm was sustained by public enterprise, and by that logic Boeing does owe the public some return. Part of that is jobs, part of that is taxes. Public enterprise also allows Boeing the luxury of being able to externalize its mistakes and the vagaries of the business cycle in the form of layoffs. The difficulty Airbus Industrie has had in adding workers (because of government regulations, it has a difficult time laying them off, so it hires only sparingly, making it harder to boost production on up-cycles) bears loud testimony to how important a gift that is to Boeing. In short, there must be a balance between public and private needs.

In the case of Seattle and Washington State, nothing so drastic as paying Boeing seems necessary. The region has only to meet Boeing's marginal propensity to move—make sure the costs of staying are just lower than the costs of moving. Without selling its soul, the region could pave the way for local construction of both superjumbo and supersonic jetliners (Boeing's two most likely upcoming projects), if only by forcing itself to deal with both the permitting process and the infrastructure question. (Why not volunteer to get on the federal military base-closure list and turn McChord Air Force Base into an aero-industrial complex, producing far more in high paying jobs and tax revenues than any five or six military bases? Of course, if you even mention this in Pierce County, you will get verbally lynched. And what a shame it would be to lose all those massage parlors and rent-to-own emporia.)

Whatever the course, the region must, for a rare and lucid moment, squarely confront the Paradox of Growth. A region cannot just stop growing without assuming some rather large costs, costs that could go so high as to cause contraction. The externalities of growth will always force some hard decisions or otherwise denigrate a region's quality of life. One can find too many despoiled views, too many strip-mall scarred 'burbs where growth occurred without the burden of zoning or planning or much of anything at all. Miles of unrelenting pavement frankly is not all that attractive, and there is no reason why urban areas have to look that way.

Only government has the authority to make that happen—provide building standards, ample parks, roads and rapid transit, and room for enough housing. This requires a couple of things, not least a tax structure that allows state and local governments to use the benefits of economic growth to help pay to ameliorate the externalities. It also requires the political will to make decisions and stick with them. Faced with an unhappy Boeing, Renton and Everett switched gears to a partnership mode; that should have been the starting point.

As for Boeing, that a single organization could have such influence on public policy might lead one to ask whether this is a perversion of democracy. But as Lindblom, Petersen, and so many others have concluded, big employers are important enough to the system to justify some degree of attention from the civic infrastructure. In some ways, the sentiment that any group of citizens should have as much influence as a Boeing is morally attractive but practically silly. The bottom line is that for most of us the Boeings will be more significant and have more impact than we will. Understandably the governor is going to return Phil Condit's phone calls a lot sooner than he is going to return ours.

Nonetheless, few of us who are not big business executives would like to see big business run the country. The chief virtue of the many small groups that opposed Boeing in the 1990s may have been largely to keep the company honest, exercising that faction-on-faction friction that James Madison saw as so essential in a functioning republic.[26]

The more immediate issue is not Boeing, however. For Washington State, at least, it is everybody else. In 1996, Ron Woodard, president of Boeing Commercial Airplane Group, spoke at a Greater Seattle Chamber of Commerce function, much like the one that Shrontz had spoken at five years before. In his speech, he repeated Boeing's traditional themes. "It's not easy or user friendly to get something built here," Woodard said. He expressed Boeing's continuing concerns about moving parts up and down the Interstate 5 corridor between Everett and Tacoma, and about the continuing viability of Seattle-Tacoma International Airport. He touted the one million hours of time Boeing employees had donated to charity in 1995, and called for wider access to higher education. But afterward, speaking to reporters, Woodard allowed that plant expansion was no longer an issue. "We've already built everything we can build," he said. "My problem now is using everything efficiently."

Away from the speech, someone asked casually about his vacation home on Shaw Island, in Washington's picturesque San Juan archipelago. Woodard sighed. He lamented the difficulty of getting a permit to build a dock on his family's recently acquired retreat. Some 120 of his neighbors were opposing the dock, including his four nearest neighbors, each of whom had a dock. Woodard said he had, at that point, spent more on legal fees than it would have cost to build the dock. "I don't think we'll get it built," he said.

Whatever the virtues of his proposed dock, his plight underscores the difficulty of balancing growth and preservation. It is not the Ron Woodards and Boeings who are in peril; it is the small firms and sole proprietorships, the next Boeings, whose businesses falter or fail because they are hampered by regulation. Boeing has resources. It can take care of itself.

But a balance has to be struck. Unfettered growth would be no better than an all-constricting growth management; the previously unzoned Lynn-woods and Federal Ways of Western Washington, featuring mile after mile of traffic-snarled strip malls, bear garish testimony to what doing nothing about growth can achieve. Our hope must be for a middle ground that is sometimes paved, sometimes green. Finding that ground should be among the first tasks of the new century.

Epilogue

Growth and Antigrowth, Revisited

The ingredients for all possible outcomes have been and remain visible
in modern Washington. Washington seems forever to be in a state of
becoming.

—Neal R. Pierce and Jerry Hagstrom, 1984

TO WORK OUR WAY OUT of the Paradox of Growth, we must go back.
Barring a true Hobbesian state of nature, goods and services will be produced in human society, or we'll all die. We may organize this production in several fashions, chiefly along a continuum ranging from complete
collectivization to utter atomization, with either end of the spectrum
promising some degree of chaos despite utopian aims and promises. It is
a frequent fault of human philosophy (and public policy) to equate goals
with outcomes.

Human society is based in part on the production of goods and services,
a notion well understood by both Adam Smith and Karl Marx. For Marx,
however, it was the act of working that was central. Work has its own
intrinsic rewards, but it also is a means to an end. The first human who
learned to chip stones for bonking bunnies knew this. And when someone
learned to do it a little better, he could trade those stones for surplus com-
modities produced by his neighbors. So commerce was born. As soon as
society organized beyond the family level, government—a formalized over-
structure intended to optimize production and distribution of resources—
sought to control and skim the cream from that productivity (a habit evident in governments from the mercantilism of eighteenth-century Europe
to the crony capitalism of twentieth-century Asia). It was not until Adam
Smith wrote it down that we accepted the notion that perhaps more wealth
could be produced by getting government out of the way.

Smith anticipated that there would be externalities, that capitalism by itself might fail to provide public goods such as roads and schools. Over time, the externalities magnified, and the very greed that capitalist theory and practice seek to optimize led capitalists to bury competitors, gouge customers, and enslave employees, all the while devastating the one thing we're not making any more of—land. And so regulation of a new kind arose, a kind that seeks to mitigate the negative externalities that business so often generates.

Inequality certainly is not the least of these externalities. Modern liberal democratic capitalism has produced a remarkable amount of wealth in widely uneven dispersal. And that can create problems: "If the concentrated resources of the great corporations can be readily translated into disproportionate political power, it is difficult to see how citizens with no corporate connections will have much influence when corporations decide to contest a political issue. No other private actors can match the wealth of these huge enterprises."[1]

In modern society, business and government together organize the production of goods and services. In any economy with any degree of freedom, business will have power because of the central role it plays in that function. Power tends to centralize over time; once one has it, one tries to protect it and get more of it. When power centralizes, its wielders tend to exclude others from the benefits that accrue.

That kind of power threatens society in myriad ways: "Corporate discretion poses an increasingly serious threat to popular control as the business enterprise grows in size," Charles Lindblom wrote. "The discretionary decision of a single large corporation (to move in or out) can create or destroy a town, pollute the air for an entire city, upset the balance of payments between countries, and wipe out the livelihoods of thousands of employees."[2]

The assumption here is that wealth equals power; it is probably safer to say that it is a necessary but incomplete ingredient, like oxygen to fire. Wealth can buy things: media time, sweet-tongued spokespersons and lobbyists, access through campaign contributions. Such initiatives need be only marginally successful to lend an air of disproportionality to the political efforts of business. But to argue that business has otherworldly power simply because it spends more money is to suggest that the state pays no attention to anything but money. And nobody who has ever tried to get a short-plat in King County has come away thinking that all you need is cash.

Any government official who understands the requirements of his position and the responsibilities that market-oriented systems throw on businessmen will therefore grant them a privileged position. He does not have to be bribed, duped or pressured to do so. Nor does he have to be an uncritical admirer of businessmen to do so. He simply understands, as is plain to see, that public affairs in market-oriented systems are in the hands of two groups of leaders, government and business, who must collaborate, and that to make the system work government leadership often must defer to business leadership. Collaboration and deference between the two are at the heart of politics in such systems.[3]

Everyone relies on a healthy economy, but business does not always get what it wants. Business interests often have significant power and influence, but they are not alone. Governments also have power: witness their ability to promulgate regulations and procedures that businesses find abhorrent, however they may learn to live with them. Bureaucrats have leverage over elites in suggesting agendas, providing technical expertise, or just getting in the way.[4]

This ragged, shifting, uneven, yet functional balance of power slows down the policy process, sometimes to a groping crawl. Of course, that was the intent of the federalist system. It will eventually force compromise. And compromise is what we need.

Things change. In 1997, Boeing officially merged with (and unofficially acquired) McDonnell Douglas, whose commercial business was all but gone but whose military business was thriving. The personal fallout took time to develop, but eventually Bud Coffey's heir apparent, Rob Makin, was ushered out the door. The initial rumor was that the new governor, Gary Locke, could not stand him—which may very well have been true—but ultimately it may have been simply a case of who got along with whom at corporate headquarters. Makin apparently landed on his feet, however, and at last report was thriving as a contract lobbyist for a fistful of clients.[5]

Whatever the state of his dock, Ron Woodard also felt the axe in 1998, as fall guy for mounting production problems in the Commercial Airplane Group he headed. In 1997 Boeing posted its first annual loss since before dirt, as it wrote off the cost of playing catch-up with a record number of orders. It was hard to say whether Woodard was to blame. People who knew him on the shop floor were not always very positive about their encounters.

People who knew him as a salesman, however, said there was none better. One summer, when I ran into him aboard a ferry, each of us on our way to the San Juans, I found him cordial, friendly, and like most people who travel a lot, dog tired.

Meanwhile, the problem of growth again breached the surface in the late 1990s. As the state's economy boomed, so did growth. For three straight years through 1996, Washington was the third-fastest growing state in the country.[6] The *Seattle Times,* National Public Radio station KUOW, and PBS TV affiliate KCTS combined forces for the oddly named "Front Porch Forum,"[7] in which they purported to plumb the depths of public feeling about growth. The results were predictable: most people said they did not like the burdens of growth—the traffic, the rising cost of housing, the pollution, and the loss of open space. Few of the participants seemed to understand what tradeoffs were involved in growth management (such as the difficulty of maintaining an affordable housing stock while putting limits on new housing—that their children would be less likely to be able afford to live here as a result of curbs on growth). Yet many offered the usual set of last-man-over-the-drawbridge responses involving various restrictions on new development. There were calls in one gathering to stop migration into the United States. At least one person spoke fondly of the Boeing Bust.[8]

Civic leaders also took up the call, and opposition was loud and persistent to efforts to bring the 2012 Summer Olympic Games to Seattle—both in and outside of government.[9] For the growth and its costs were fairly obvious. King County's annual growth report showed that while population increased 1 percent (to 1.68 million in 1999), housing prices rose 16 percent and rents rose 8 percent. Salmon numbers were down in local watersheds, and county residents were making more money and driving farther to do it.[10] King County executive Ron Sims, certainly an advocate of affordable housing, nonetheless said the county should continue with growth management and stop development in rural areas.[11]

The growth came even as Boeing was creeping toward the next aerospace downcycle. Layoffs returned, although not in numbers as large as in the past. Aerospace continued to be the region's largest private employer, but payroll in software actually exceeded aerospace payroll in 1999 (buoyed by the generous stock options many software workers enjoyed).[12] Some people I talked to took that headline to mean that *employment* in the software industry had surpassed that of aerospace, and they cannot have been alone. It only serves to underscore the public perception that Boeing just is not as important anymore.

Someday, perhaps in the next decade, Boeing will build a new product, and it is hard to imagine the company having an easy time expanding in the Puget Sound region when that time comes.[13] The region is likely to continue to grow, the sprawl spreading north and south along Interstate 5 while local officials pat themselves on the back for having commissioned more studies on how to deal with it. The prospect of another Boeing plant will offer mixed blessings, welcome only if the economy is in the tank. I think that being one of the world's aerospace capitals has been economically good for the region. (And ultimately culturally good, because the wealth of aircraft, in part, has made possible the wealth of artistic endeavor that the region enjoys.) It will be sad to see that pass. But that is the Paradox of Growth: we work like serfs to fatten the goose, and then when it gets too big, we try to wring its neck.

Some things don't change. The business community headed into the new millennium with its usual complaints, but with no greater understanding of what might be driving them. In 1995, the Washington Roundtable released a report, *Principles for Prosperity: How Washington's Business Climate Compares. How Washington Must Change to Compete.* It was a curious piece of work. It contained the usual pablum about how lousy it was to do business in Washington State: "Public policy decisions at all levels of government have made Washington state an expensive place to do business," citing health care legislation, the Growth Management Act, and "a very tough State Environmental Policy Act."[14]

The panel, a collection of thirty-two CEOs from the state's biggest companies, called for creating "attitudes supportive of economic prosperity for businesses and households," with a government to "champion a culture ... which recognizes a link between the cost of doing business, job creation and the ability to pay taxes." They repeated the call for streamlining the regulatory process, decrying the fact that "local governments now exercise regulatory authority over telecommunications, growth management, consumer protection and many other areas that affect our competitive position."[15]

But while bemoaning the Evergreen State as "a costly place to do business," the CEOs called for more "investment" in education, and more spending for infrastructure and basic services such as sewers and public safety (the money for this to come from who knows where).[16] While on the one hand the Roundtable declared that the region enjoyed a strong quality of life, at the same time it belittled the state's overall business climate, citing numbers that put the state in the bottom quarter nationally for business while ranking high in taxes and wages. (Several of the CEOs, according to their firms' own annual proxy statements, made more than $1 million a year. How anyone who makes more than six figures can complain about his employees' high wages is completely beyond me.)

Closer examination of the numbers underscores just how difficult is the balance between public and private needs, however. The states that scored highly in business climate factors generally scored abysmally in quality of life factors. Could all this regulation and these unfairly high wages actually have something to do with quality of life? The notion escaped the CEOs, who seem to want the benefits of Washington and the costs of Mississippi (great business-climate scores, bottom-rung quality-of-life scores).

The Roundtable repeated its effort the following year with *Preparing for Washington's High-Tech Future,* in which, confound them, 57 percent of high-tech executives rated Washington as a good or excellent place to do business. Only 7 percent rated it "poor" or "failing." Despite that, the report restated the laundry list of ills unveiled in 1995.[17] More interesting, perhaps, was that the state's high-tech firms were mostly homegrown, thriving despite the state having downgraded its efforts to recruit plants from other states.

Harvard business professor Rosabeth Moss Kanter, in one of those precious drive-by analyses of Seattle, saw this as a problem. "Seattle struggles with the proper balance between protecting its environment and saving jobs by changing what business leaders on my survey [sic] called an unwieldy regulatory apparatus and slow permitting process that could cause companies to leave the area," she wrote. "It aspires to be an international city, but its economic development strategy focuses largely on indigenous entrepreneurs rather than attracting international investment to the city."[18]

Fostering homegrown entrepreneurs would seem to have some advantages: (1) it costs less public money to nurture them, and (2) they are less likely to leave once they achieve success. Burlington Northern once relocated its headquarters to Seattle, then left for a better offer elsewhere. Companies such as Boeing, Microsoft, and Immunex, for example, should be less likely to pack up and move to Houston, Denver, or Orlando (if we don't chase them away). Moreover, active recruiting of more business—if at all successful—likely will spur the Paradox of Growth, generating costs for existing residents and businesses.

As the century ended, Seattle was not alone in its concern about growth. As early as 1988, communities in California were seriously wrestling with the costs of growth.[19] At least a dozen states and cities had growth management legislation in place, and more than two hundred growth management measures appeared on ballots nationwide in 1998. In Colorado, for example, growth became the prime issue in places such as Aspen. "What's indisputable is the current scenario: Out-of-sight real estate prices, supposedly inflated by growth control begun in the 1970s, have forced 55 percent of Aspen's employees to live in nearby towns. 'Aspenization' is the term for this—the squeezing of the top of the balloon until the bottom expands."[20]

And yet few people seem to understand the Paradox. University of Washington geographer Richard Morrill, in a commentary so insightful it was sure to have been ignored, pointed out what should be obvious: successful growth controls would have to be severe, and they would have consequences.

> So the ONLY [emphasis in original] way to reduce growth significantly is to make the region less attractive and hospitable by creating and maintaining FEWER JOBS and to reduce our appeal to those not concerned with jobs. This would not be easy, but it may be possible. Essentially, the state (Legislature) of Washington would have to direct the counties and cities of the relevant area (King, Pierce, Snohomish, Kitsap, Thurston?) that permits could not be issued for new plant and office capacity or utility hookups that would lead to increased hiring above some threshold.... Such drastic intervention in the private economy is probably not constitutional in the U.S.... A far less palatable and riskier way to slow job growth would be to raise taxes, fees and regulations on business. While this would discourage new entry of firms, it would equally penalize existing firms and probably drive many out of business.[21]

Morrill went on to note that merely slowing the pace of expansion, or imposing building moratoria, likely will drive up housing prices. Such a strategy "only works if there are lots of nearby jurisdictions that don't try to control growth."[22]

And lots of jurisdictions were trying to control growth. Denver and Salt Lake City were studying it, and calls were rising in Phoenix and Las Vegas, as well as in British Columbia, Colorado, Massachusetts, Pennsylvania, and Minnesota. New Jersey, Michigan, California, Florida, Maine, Vermont,

Rhode Island, Georgia, Tennessee, Maryland, and South Carolina (cele-brated at length by Kanter for its success in attracting European manufac-turing firms) had growth management legislation on the books. Portland and San Jose had urban growth boundaries, and even burgeoning Atlanta was being forced to think about growth, if only by federal air pollution laws.[23] Wherever quality of life issues arise, concern about growth follows, even in a conservative state such as Idaho.[24] (And yet other regions con-tinue to pursue growth at high costs, such as bids as high as $40 million in incentives for an America Online operations center, and $155 million for a 300-job steel mill. That's $517,333 a job—why not just give the money away?)[25]

Some have suggested growth controls can work, distinguishing between NIMBYism (Not in My Back Yard)[26] and "regional growth management."[27] But even in what appears to be a sensible, longstanding, and highly re-garded growth management program—the city of Portland, Oregon's—housing prices ultimately began to rise,[28] meaning growth was just being pushed off somewhere else.

This is the Paradox of Growth. After centuries of promoting growth, we find that we can have too much; discouraging growth can mean we not only stop growing but start contracting, losing the growth we tried so hard to get in the first place.

The private sector's understanding of the Paradox may be no greater than the public sector's. In a near perfect bookend to the century-opening (1921) speech by some now-forgotten Boeing executive, Boeing CFO Debby Hopkins closed the era with yet another harangue about how awful it is to do business in Washington State. Speaking to the Greater Seattle Chamber of Commerce, Hopkins extolled the virtues of the region's natural beauty—the mountains, the rolling wheatfields, the rivers. "Yet none is as remark-able as sailing through the San Juans at sunset, watching whales breach next to our boat." And yet, moments later, she could repeat the age-old complaint that "our labor costs in Washington are among the highest in the nation."[29] Last time I checked, sailing through the San Juans was not exactly a cheap hobby. Decades of paying workers a living wage and treat-ing them with respect helped Boeing to become the world's dominant aerospace firm, but that notion seems to be slipping away from the com-pany's executives.

Moreover, the genesis of their concerns appeared to be lost on company executives as well. While complaining about labor and transportation costs,

Hopkins also said the state was not doing enough to recruit high-tech businesses. If you think this through, it makes no sense. Recruiting more firms to come to Washington would spur growth, which would further tax infrastructure—one of Boeing's chief concerns. It would also further bid up the price of wages, as companies competed for available labor. Both of these things happened during the growth cycle of the 1990s. Other things that Hopkins mentioned—improving schools, controlling unemployment insurance costs, preserving the ability of local governments to raise taxes to address infrastructure problems—are all sensible. But unless the state can get high-tech firms to locate in historically distressed areas (which is not very likely), attracting new businesses is probably not the answer to managing the Paradox of Growth. And it is the Paradox that is at the heart of Boeing's—and everybody else's—long list of complaints.

Solutions will be difficult and unlikely to please everyone, or perhaps anyone. Restrictions on development will raise housing and land prices. Higher taxes, in whatever form, for whatever reason, will be borne by all, not just by newcomers. Greater environmental restrictions will spread costs and benefits broadly but unevenly across the landscape.

What are to be avoided are Draconian measures that do more harm than good, and we should not underestimate the ability of human beings to think them up. Greater state control of the economy may seem very out of vogue at the dawn of the new millennium, but it is an alternative that will rise again in some form or another. And whatever you call it—Marxism, socialism, statism—it carries significant costs of its own.

The reader should not underestimate what can be done by statists in free-market clothing. In 1999, some local officials criticized the city of Federal Way for not "taking" more of its share of housing (the city was not growing as dictated by growth management plans). At least one group asked the legislature to allow counties to levy sanctions against local cities that did not meet growth targets. Federal Way, a city of 70,000 and itself a victim of unplanned growth, has terrible traffic, no discernible downtown, and is not very convenient to any job that is not nearby. The city mayor's protestations that people simply were not moving there did not seem to draw much sympathy. If such sanctions were approved and utilized, would the city then have to entice builders and homebuyers to build and move there? All to preserve somebody else's rural splendor?[30]

Greater state control of economic development would end the competition between regions for factories and jobs. Ostensibly, factories would only be sited in places where it made sense for them to be (politics could not possibly enter into such decisions, could they). As usual, there are costs. Greater state control of the economy will curb if not stifle entrepreneurship and innovation. Statism ignores the role of the capitalist, especially the part of the entrepreneur, in the creation of wealth, assuming instead a nearly static level of production with no reference to the role of human motivation in producing goods and services beyond mere subsistence. A major problem with capitalism is centralization of power, as modern statists often argue. And yet any statist solution runs the same risk, because weakening the private sector necessarily strengthens the state, removing sources of opposition that keep state power in check. Assuming that an unopposed state will be completely altruistic is about as naïve a notion as has ever been suggested, and yet statism ultimately rests on this hope.

Leftist critics do have some trenchant complaints about the power of the wealthy. Elites have more money, but are they too powerful? Perhaps. Limiting the power of any group or class also is not without cost: there is a huge bargain to be struck between efficiency and equality. Equality is inclusive; efficiency is productive. Striking a balance is the hard part. Each step along the continuum represents a substantial trade-off. We could institute "strong democracy," such as neighborhood councils with real teeth.[31] If you like complete stasis, this could be your game.[32] Moreover, limiting private power necessarily enhances state power, removing the factional conflict that is the only thing that makes our federal system of government work. This is an extraordinary cost, and it cannot be overlooked. No market will function properly without a government to ensure that it operates freely, and no government will remain democratic without countervailing forces with the resources to adequately oppose it. The state and the capitalist are partners on the same team, and it is time for all of the players to realize it.

The Paradox of Growth can only be solved through what promises to be wrenching and painful compromise. What is called for is growth planning as opposed to growth management. Most growth-control regulations call for some estimation of what growth will be, and growth is a very difficult thing to predict. Growth planners would instead say, "This is the amount of development we can tolerate, and where and how much we're going to grow." Housing and commercial developments and the infrastructure to serve them would be sited ahead of time. The costs would have to be widely distributed, through a tax structure that allowed communities to capture the benefits of growth. Such decisions would likely provoke an outcry from landowners who hoped to subdivide and sell (most of whom have completely lost sight of the idea that one gets a return on one's investment by assuming some risk). And by saying, "These are the limits," costs would be raised. This is inescapable. On the other hand, the costs would be predictable and finite.

Clearly, there are no simple solutions, no easy answers. We will not get something for nothing when it comes to managing growth, despite all the wishful thinking that marks the arguments of advocates on both sides of the debate. Any choice we make will mean that some tradeoffs also will be made. The reader should not conclude that the author is either pro- or antigrowth; I'm neither.[33] All I ask—what anyone should ask—is that we look a little farther in making those tradeoffs.

Notes

PREFACE

1. I was not especially good at framing questions. I recall asking one particularly cheery fellow how gasoline prices got set. "How should I know?" he yelled. "That's like asking me who runs the country."

PROLOGUE

1. For their idea of "nondecisions," see Peter Bachrach and Morton S. Baratz, "Decisions and Nondecisions: An Analytical Framework," in Aiken and Mott, pp. 308–20. See also Bachrach and Baratz, "Two Faces of Power," in Nivola and Rosenbloom, pp. 142–51.

2. See, for example, James O'Connor, *The Fiscal Crisis of the State* (New York: St. Martin's Press, 1973); and Ira Katznelson, *City Trenches: Urban Politics and the Patterning of Class in the United States* (New York: Pantheon Books, 1981).

3. See, for example, John R. Logan and Harvey L. Molotch, *Urban Fortunes: The Political Economy of Place* (Berkeley: University of California Press, 1987); and G. William Domhoff, "The Growth Machine and the Power Elite: A Challenge to Pluralists and Marxists Alike," and Thomas R. Dye, "Community Power and Public Policy," in *Waste*, pp. 53–75 and 29–51.

4. Logan and Molotch, p. 13. Domhoff, to cite another example, is giddy over the alleged hegemony of the growth machine: "Growth machine. It has a ring to it. It is one of those concepts at once dramatic and insightful that is immediately grasped because it captures so much of our experience and reading. It deserves to take its place alongside 'the power elite' as one of the key orienting concepts of power structure research" (p. 58).

5. Domhoff, p. 62.

6. Ibid., pp. 63–68. Logan and Molotch blithely generalize from every confirming case, but when faced with other results, such as when the growth machine fails to achieve its ends, they caution that it is "important ... not to overgeneralize these cases to the whole country" (p. 159). Furthermore, if elites really do run cities, why have they allowed so many to decline and suffer through fiscal fiascoes such as have been experienced in Cleveland and New York? See John J. Harrigan, *Political Change in the Metropolis* (New York: Harper Collins, 1993), p. 215.

7. Dye, p. 35.

8. Richard Edward DeLeon, *Left Coast City: Progressive Politics in San Francisco, 1975–1991* (Lawrence: University Press of Kansas, 1992), pp. 2–3.

9. Ibid., pp. 40–41.

10. Ibid., p. 56.

11. Robert A. Dahl, "Rethinking *Who Governs?*: New Haven Revisited," in *Waste* (1986), p. 184. Moreover, cities are not broadly pluralist, or why would so many minority groups and even some businesses be excluded from decision making? See Harrigan, p. 215. As E. E. Schattschneider put it, "The flaw in the pluralist heaven is that the heavenly choir sings with a strong upper-class accent" (*The Semi-Sovereign People: A Realist's View of Democracy in America* [New York: Holt, Rinehart and Winston, 1960], p. 35).

12. Others have suggested that power has yet a "third face" in which the less powerful are so completely dominated that they do not raise even issues that might seem obvious to an outsider. If a group of people were being told not to educate their children, for example, with the result that each generation produced a docile pool of cheap labor, most of us would agree that the group's real interests were being hidden from them. But questions of political economy are rarely that simple. John Gaventa's coal miners were indeed shabbily treated for nearly a century by the mine owners, but who are we to ascribe their ambivalence to being deluded by more powerful interests? See Steven Lukes, *Power: A Radical View* (London: Macmillan, 1974); and Gaventa, *Power and Powerlessness: Quiescence and Rebellion in an Appalachian Valley* (Urbana: University of Illinois Press, 1980). In big steel towns such as Gary, Indiana, despite the severity of air pollution, anti–air pollution activists did not raise public support for the issue in part because of the jobs that could be at stake if the steel company was forced to shoulder pollution control costs. Seen Matthew A. Crenson, *The Un-politics of Air Pollution: A Study of Non-decisionmaking in the Cities* (Baltimore: Johns Hopkins University Press, 1971). One might argue that the steel company has hoodwinked the town, but if it were your

job and your air, what would you decide? It may be easier to choose when it is not your livelihood that is on the line.

13. Bryan D. Jones and Lynn W. Bachelor, *The Sustaining Hand: Community Leadership and Corporate Power* (Lawrence: University Press of Kansas, 1993), p. xi; see also Stanley L. Elkin, *City and Regime in the American Republic* (Chicago: University of Chicago Press, 1987), p. 8.

14. Peter K. Eisinger, *The Rise of the Entrepreneurial State* (Madison: University of Wisconsin Press, 1988), p. 34.

15. Elkin, p. 31.

16. Jones and Bachelor, p. 8.

17. Like Logan and Molotch, Jones and Bachelor question whether all the effort is worth it; it was not clear, for instance, if Detroit's investment in keeping General Motors in town would pay for itself in tax revenues. But it is possible—and this is the unasked question in most research—that while things might not be better with the plant, they might be worse without it.

18. Jones and Bachelor, p. 18.

19. Ibid., p. 231.

20. Graham K. Wilson, *Business and Politics: A Comparative Introduction* (Chatham, N.J.: Chatham House Publishers, 1990), p. 5.

21. Graham T. Allison, *Essence of Decision: Explaining the Cuban Missile Crisis* (Boston: Little, Brown, 1971).

22. John H. Mollenkopf, *The Contested City* (Princeton, N.J.: Princeton University Press, 1983).

23. See Elkin; and Clarence N. Stone, "Power and Social Complexity," in *Waste* (1986), pp. 77–113.

24. Jones and Bachelor, p. 12.

25. Harrigan, p. 219.

26. Charles Edward Lindblom, *Politics and Markets: The World's Political Economic Systems* (New York: Basic Books, 1977), pp. 206–7.

27. Dahl found that in nineteenth-century New Haven business was government. See *Who Governs? Democracy and Power in an American City* (New Haven: Yale University Press, 1961, pp. 11–31).

28. David Reisman, *The Lonely Crowd* (New Haven: Yale University Press, 1950), pp. 206–7. By 1960, Dahl finds among New Haven's patricians a disdain for manufacturing, the same patricians who by then have the time and inclination to take up politics as a career ("From Oligarchy to Pluralism: The Patricians and the Entrepreneurs," in Aiken and Mott, pp. 31–32. Robert O. Schulze found similar results

elsewhere; see "The Role of Economic Dominants in Community Power Structure," in Aiken and Mott, p. 62.

29. See Robert Mills French, "Economic Change and Community Power Structures: Transition in Cornucopia," in Aiken and Mott, pp. 180–89; Donald A. Clelland and William H. Form, "Economic Dominants and Community Power: A Comparative Analysis," in Aiken and Mott, pp. 66–77; and Schulze.

30. DeLeon, p. 53.

31. David Easton, *A Framework for Political Analysis* (Englewood Cliffs, N.J.: Prentice-Hall, 1965), p. 50.

32. Todd G. Buchholz, *New Ideas from Dead Economists: An Introduction to Modern Economic Thought* (New York: Penguin Books, 1990), pp. 35–36.

33. Robert A. Leone, *Who Profits: Winners, Losers, and Government Regulation* (New York: Basic Books, 1986), p. 3.

34. See Stone, p. 83.

35. Ibid., pp. 84, 87.

36. Richard C. Berner, *Seattle, 1900–1920* (Seattle: Charles Press, 1991), p. 9.

37. Clive Thomas and Ronald J. Hrebenar, "Interest Groups in the States," in Gray, et al., p. 142. Thomas and Hrebenar list Boeing as among a half dozen prominent interests in Washington State (p. 567).

38. Boeing's experience on the federal level is a perfect example of the Third Law. Throughout the 1960s, '70s, and '80s, the company lost military contracts despite products that were technologically and financially superior (such as its design for the C-5 military cargo aircraft) to firms with better political connections. Firms such as Lockheed, which won the C-5 contract in the 1960s and a follow-up contract in the 1980s, had bigger pull in Congress because they had operations in more politically important areas such as California and Atlanta (where the right committee chairman resided and where some C-5 work landed). But when Boeing rose to become the nation's leading exporter and its leading symbol of technological competence, it had much more luck in getting the government to support open trade with big clients such as China, as well as support in battles over European subsidies to Airbus Industrie.

CHAPTER 1 / THE RUNWAY

1. Bill Richards, "Boeing May Go Elsewhere for New Jets," *Seattle Post-Intelligencer*, Sept. 21, 1991, pp. A1, A4.

2. Glenn Pascall, Douglas H. Pedersen, and Richard S. Conway, *The Boeing Company Economic Impact Study* (Seattle: Boeing Company, 1987), p. 7.

3. Sarah McCally Morehouse, *State Politics, Parties, and Policy* (New York: Holt, Rinehart and Winston, 1981). Frustratingly, she does not say much about how she arrived at this conclusion.

4. "Et in Cascadia, Ego," *The Economist*, Feb. 29, 1992, p. 29.

5. Gar Alperovitz and Jeff Faux, "Think Again: What We Need Is More Government, Not Less," *Washington Post*, National Weekly Edition, Oct. 22, 1984, p. 21.

6. Jürgen Habermas, *Legitimation Crisis* (New York: Beacon Press, 1990); the Paradox of Growth is, to my mind, precisely the kind of thing Habermas is talking about. Of course, Habermas and Moynihan come down on different sides of the issue. Habermas's answer is some sort of Marxism whereas Moynihan's is balance and restraint. Fortunately, Habermas never got elected to the U.S. Senate.

7. "The Social Responsibility of Business," in Daniel P. Moynihan, *Business and Society in Change* (New York: AT&T, 1975), p. 14.

8. Theodore J. Lowi, *The End of Liberalism: The Second Republic of the United States* (New York: W. W. Norton, 1979), pp. 5–6.

9. See, for example, Logan and Molotch.

CHAPTER 2 / COME FLY WITH US

1. Harold Mansfield, *Vision: The Story of Boeing* (New York: Popular Press, 1966), p. 11.

2. *Aberdeen Daily World*, "W. E. Boeing, Plane Company Founder, Called," September 29, 1956, p. 1.

3. Mansfield, p. 9.

4. Gerald B. Nelson, *Seattle: The Life and Times of an American City* (New York: Alfred A. Knopf, 1977), pp. 30–31.

5. Mrs. Sutton Gustison, "The Boeing Story," *Pacific Northwest Quarterly*, April 1954, p. 41

6. *Aberdeen Daily World*, September 29, 1956, p. 1.

7. David Brewster and David M. Buerge, *Washingtonians: A Biographical Portrait of the State* (Seattle: Sasquatch Books, 1988), p. 180

8. E. E. Bauer, *Boeing in Peace and War* (Enumclaw, Wash.: TABA Publishing, 1990), p. xiii.

9. Ibid., pp. 15–16

10. Eugene Rodgers, *Flying High* (New York: Atlantic Monthly Press, 1996), pp. 466–68.

11. See Robert W. Lotchin, *Fortress California, 1910–1961* (New York: Oxford University Press, 1992).

12. Edwin J. Cohn, Jr., *Industry in the Pacific Northwest and the Location Theory* (New York: King's Crown Press, 1954), p. 3.

13. See Roger Sale, *Seattle, Past to Present* (Seattle: University of Washington Press, 1976), chapter 2; and Nelson, p. 6.

14. Washington State Local Governance Study Commission, *A History of Washington's Local Governments: Final Report*, Volume 1 (Olympia, Wash.: The Commission, Institute of Public Policy, The Evergreen State College, 1988), p. 3.

15. Ibid.

16. Kenneth M. Dolbeare, *Economic Development and Jobs in Washington: A Citizen's Guide* (Olympia, Wash.: The Evergreen State College, 1983), p. 3.

17. Berner (1991), pp. 10–11.

18. Kenneth Dolbeare, *The Evolution of the Public Sector in Washington State* (Olympia: The Evergreen State College, 1988), p. 19. Dolbeare is not alone in making a strong case that citizens' anger at the railroads led to the peculiarities of the state's constitution, such as the multiple layers of government. The state, he notes, has more special-purpose districts per capita than any other place in the country. "Washington's district fetish is the principal residue of its radical period" (p. 1). It also resulted in the state constitution prohibiting the lending of public credit to any company or individual (p. 23).

19. Ibid., p. 30.

20. Cohn, p. 26.

21. Berner (1991), p. 22.

22. Dolbeare (1983), p. 10.

23. Daniel Jack Chasan and Heather Doran Barbieri, *Seattle: World Class City* (Seattle: Windsor Publications, 1991), p. 33.

24. Richard C. Berner, *Seattle, 1921–1940* (Seattle: Charles Press, 1992), pp. 175–76.

25. Lotchin, p. 66.

26. Berner (1992), pp. 435–36.

27. Bauer, p. 101.

28. James C. Collins and Jerry I. Porras, *Built to Last: Successful Habits of Visionary Companies* (New York: Harper Collins, 1997), p. 61.

29. Bauer, pp. 22–26.

30. John McCann, *Blood in the Water: A History of District Lodge 751, IAM&AW* (Seattle: District Lodge 751, 1989), pp. 46–47. Local union leadership voted to admit blacks in 1940, but those leaders were replaced in an internal power struggle, and the new group voted to rescind that decision. District Lodge 751, as the Boeing group became known, started campaigning for inclusion of nonwhites as early as

1945, but it took longer to convince the American Federation of Labor's national leadership (pp. 47–49).

31. Except Karl Sabbagh, *Twenty-First-Century Jet: The Making and Marketing of the Boeing 777* (New York: Scribner, 1996), p. 29.

32. Clive Irving, however, points out that Postmaster General Walter Folger Brown's so-called "spoils meetings" were publicized with daily press releases, which were largely ignored at the time. See *Wide Body: The Triumph of the 747* (New York: William Morrow, 1993), p. 32.

33. Matthew Lynn, *Birds of Prey: Boeing vs. Airbus, a Battle for the Skies* (New York: Four Walls Eight Windows, 1997), pp. 44–45.

34. Mansfield, p. 47.

35. Cynthia H. Wilson, "Emperor of the Skies: The Boeings," in Brewster and Buerge, pp. 179–86.

36. Gerald D. Nash, *World War II and the West: Reshaping the Economy* (Lincoln: University of Nebraska Press, 1990), p. 68.

37. Gerald D. Nash, *The American West Transformed: The Impact of the Second World War* (Bloomington: Indiana University Press, 1985), p. 156. This is the genesis of Airbus executives' defensive harangue about the enormous subsidy that the European consortium survived on for the first twenty years of its existence. Boeing, they say, also got a lot of help from the government on the defense side. They leave out the fact that the Airbus partners also are among the largest defense contractors in Europe and so should have enjoyed at least some of the same sort of subsidy.

38. Norbert McDonald, *Distant Neighbors: A Comparative History of Seattle and Vancouver* (Lincoln: University of Nebraska Press, 1987), p. 139.

39. Richard S. Kirkendall, "The Boeing Company and the Military-Metropolitan-Industrial Complex, 1945-1953," *Pacific Northwest Quarterly*, October 1994, p. 137.

40. Robert E. Ficken and Charles P. LeWarne, *Washington: A Centennial History* (Seattle: University of Washington Press, 1989), p. 131.

41. Belle Reeves, "War Production in Washington," in Kent D. Richards, Raymond A. Smith, Jr., and Burton J. Williams, eds., *Washington: Readings in the History of the Evergreen State* (Lawrence, Kan.: Coronado Press, 1975) pp. 283–86.

42. Ficken and LeWarne, pp. 131–32.

43. William Glenn Cunningham, *The Aircraft Industry: A Study in Industrial Location* (Los Angeles: Lorin L. Morrison, 1951), p. 84.

44. Gerald D. Nash, *The American West in the Twentieth Century: A Short History of an Urban Oasis* (Englewood Cliffs, NJ: Prentice Hall, 1973), p. 9.

45. Nash (1990), pp. 70, 72.

46. Business Executives' Research Committee, *The Impact of World War II Sub-contracting by the Boeing Airplane Company upon Pacific Northwest Manufacturing* (Seattle: University of Washington, 1995, pp. 22–24, 38. Nash (1973) counted 67 in the area (p. 208).

47. Lynn, p. 50.

48. Pacific Northwest Research Center, *Boeing Arms the Corporate Empire* (Eugene, Ore.: Dec. 1974), pp. 35–36; hereafter cited as *Boeing Arms the Corporate Empire*.

49. James R. Warren, *A Century of Seattle Business* (Bellevue, Wash.: Vernon Publications, 1989), p. 34.

50. Nash (1985), pp. 79–80.

51. Ficken and LeWarne, p. 144.

52. Kirkendall (1994), p. 138.

53. Nash (1990), p. 9.

54. Kirkendall (1994), p. 138.

55. Ibid., p. 139.

56. Nash (1990), p. 87.

57. Kirkendall (1994), p. 137.

58. Nash (1990), p. 70.

59. Lotchin, p. 191.

60. Robert J. Serling, *Legend and Legacy: The Story of Boeing and Its People* (New York: St. Martin's Press, 1992), pp. 71–72.

61. Cohn, pp. 161–62.

62. Kirkendall (1994), p. 144.

63. Nash (1990), p. 87.

64. Ibid., pp. 144–46.

65. Kirkendall (1994), p. 143.

66. McCann, pp. 96–98.

67. Jacob Vander Meulen, "West Coast Aircraft Labor and an American Military-Industrial Complex, 1935–1941," Working Paper No. 4 (Seattle: Center for Labor Studies, University of Washington, August 1996), p. 28. Vander Meulen's fascinating analysis in part blames the federal government's counter-productive contracting policies of the time for generating Douglas's and Lockheed's anti-union efforts. Some of those pressures spilled over to Boeing, forcing them to cut wages. But Donald Douglas was anti-union to his core. Boeing executives had their disagreements with the unions, but none were in Douglas's league. Vander Meulen hints that federal contracting policies nearly put Boeing under in 1938, with only World War II forcing the government to become realistic about the cost of aircraft (pp. 22–23).

68. Ibid., pp. 141–43.

69. McCann, p. 99.

70. Ibid.

71. Murray Morgan, *Skid Road: An Informal Portrait of Seattle* (Sausalito: Comstock Editions, 1978), pp. 215–65. Beck, for example, worked to cut the number of service stations and to control gas prices in Seattle (p. 253). See also Roger Sale, *Seattle: Past to Present* (Seattle: University of Washington Press, 1976), pp. 144–49.

72. McCann, pp. 138–39.

73. Ibid., pp. 153–58. Daniel M. Ogden, Jr., and Hugh A. Bone note that the state was heavily unionized then, making it at least somewhat unlikely that either measure could have passed under the best of circumstances. It is interesting that neither campaign produced any long-term ill will, however, and both appear to have become mere footnotes in the state's political history. See their *Washington Politics* (New York: New York University Press, 1960), p. 55.

74. Ibid., pp. 157–58.

75. Kirkendall (1994), p. 143.

76. Irving, pp. 363–64.

77. McCann, pp. 158–59.

78. Ibid., pp. 161–68.

79. Ibid., pp. 168–69.

80. Ficken and LeWarne, p. 144.

81. Lynn, p. 53. Boeing's board of directors launched the program in April 1952.

82. Collins and Porras, pp. 91–92

83. Bauer, pp. 161–62.

84. Gustison, p. 46.

85. Richard S. Kirkendall, "Two Senators and the Boeing Company," *Columbia*, Winter, 1997–98, p. 40.

86. Ibid., pp. 38, 41–43.

87. Lynn, pp. 94, 127–28. More ominous, perhaps, and certainly less noticed at the time, was the birth of Airbus in a small office in France on December 18, 1970.

88. Rodgers, pp. 304–5.

89. Quoted in Sabbagh, p. 31.

90. Quoted in Neal R. Peirce, *The Pacific States of America: People, Politics, and Power in Five Pacific Basin States* (New York: W. W. Norton, 1972), p. 233.

91. Ibid.

92. See Neal R. Peirce, *Citistates: How Urban America Can Prosper in a Competitive World* (Washington, D.C.: Seven Locks Press, 1993), p. 96.

93. Ibid.

94. Ibid.

95. This seems to be at the heart of where so many analysts have gone wrong. Boeing still has several dozen local subcontractors, whose contributions go unnoticed because what they do is make parts for aerospace customers. And making parts for aircraft requires a strong focus on that, because the tolerances are so precise. A bad bolt for an auto assembly might mean an ill-fitting door and an unhappy customer, but an ill-fitting door on an aircraft means a jet that comes apart in mid-air. Because these subcontractors are not well known outside of industrial circles, a number of people over the years seem to have assumed that they were not really there. While at *Valley Daily News* I knew of a couple of dozen in South King County alone, but you had to be really paying attention to even know they were there. Most had limited interest in diversifying away from aerospace, depending on how much business they were getting from Boeing. The biggest problem most had was keeping workers on when Boeing was expanding and hiring good technicians away at higher wages.

96. Daniel Jack Chasan, *The Water Link: A History of Puget Sound as a Resource* (Seattle: Washington Sea Grant Program, 1981), p. 146.

97. Puget Sound had viable shipyards then as now; this is where a more forward-thinking economic development effort might have attempted to link the yards' expertise with Boeing's and kept the project alive in a sort of flexible manufacturing network.

98. See Boeing Company, *Portfolio of Opportunities: A Study of Some Specific Programs to Provide Economic Assistance to the West Coast* (Seattle: Boeing, 1975).

99. *Boeing Arms the Corporate Empire*, pp. 32–34.

100. Serling, pp. 239–47.

101. Warren, p. 39.

102. Of course the tax structure was largely put in place long before Boeing was the big game in town; see Dolbeare (1988), pp. 65–73.

103. Sale, pp. 188–89. Recall that Nash (1990) said they were evident as early as World War II (pp. 70–72).

104. Ibid.

105. Pascall, Pedersen, and Conway, p. vi.

106. Rodgers, pp. 225–26.

107. John Newhouse, *The Sporty Game* (New York: Alfred A. Knopf, 1982), p. 108.

108. Les Gapay, "Boeing Has Jumbo Impact on Economy," *Seattle Post-Intelligencer*, Jan. 20, 1987.

109. Jane Jacobs, *Cities and the Wealth of Nations* (New York: Random House, 1984), pp. 46, 179. She also attributed the 1969–71 Boeing Bust to a decline in orders

for bombers (p. 186). This was the least of Boeing's worries, and in any case, most of the bombers were built in Wichita. Boeing did lose about 1,000 jobs from losing the B-1 contract to North American Rockwell, but gained a number of those back by performing major subcontracting work on the project; see *Boeing Arms the Corporate Empire,* p. 3. Even cancellation of federal support for the SST cost the company only about 3,000 jobs. The great bulk of the layoffs came from the plunge in orders for jetliners. Jacobs's assertion is actually a fairly common one, however, spurred in part by what I suspect is a bias against military spending.

CHAPTER 3 / FLIGHT PATH

1. Kenneth Dolbeare, *The Evolution of the Public Sector in Washington State* (Olympia: The Evergreen State College, 1988), p. 7.

2. Ibid., p. 56.

3. Ibid., pp. 80–81.

4. Nash (1985), pp. 79–80

5. Sharon Boswell and Lorraine McConaghy, "Doing the Dirty Work—A Region Ravaged by Rapid Growth Sounds the Call to Clean the Water, Clear the Air," *Seattle Times,* Sept. 15, 1996.

6. Hugh A. Bone, "The Political Setting," in Thor Swanson, William F. Mullen, John C. Pierce, and Charles H. Sheldon, eds., *Political Life in Washington: Governing the Evergreen State* (Pullman: Washington State University Press, 1985), p. 2.

7. L. Harmon Ziegler and Henrik van Dalen, "Interest Groups in State Politics," in Herbert Jacob and Kenneth N. Vines, eds., *Politics in the American States* (Boston: Little, Brown, 1976), p. 95.

8. William F. Mullen and John C. Pierce, "Political Parties," in Swanson et al., pp. 55–73.

9. Elazar, cited in Elizabeth Walker, "Interest Groups in Washington State," in David C. Nice, John C. Pierce, and Charles H. Sheldon. eds., *Government and Politics in the Evergreen State* (Pullman: Washington State University Press, 1992), pp. 43–44.

10. Ziegler and van Dalen, p. 95.

11. Walker, pp. 46, 47.

12. Peirce (1972), p. 229

13. Delbert C. Miller, "Industry and Community Power Structures: A Comparative Study of an American and an English City," *American Sociological Review,* February 1958; rpt. in Aiken and Mott, p. 415.

14. Dolbeare (1983), pp. 2–3.

15. Berner (1991), p. 17.

16. Cohn, pp. 174–75.

17. Ogden and Bone, p. 10.

18. Ibid.

19. Dolbeare (1983), p. 36.

20. Ernest S. Starkman, "Imposed Constraints on the Auto Industry: A View from Two Perspectives," in S. Prakash Sethi, ed., *The Unstable Ground: Corporate Social Policy in a Dynamic Society* (Los Angeles: Melville Publishing, 1974), p. 328.

21. John E. Logan and Arthur B. Moore, Jr., "Better Decision Making in Ecological Disputes," in Sethi, p. 362.

22. Logan and Moore, pp. 362–64.

23. Dolbeare (1988), p. 112.

24. Washington State Local Governance Study Commission, *A Growth Strategy for Washington State* (Seattle: 1990), pp. 36–37.

25. Edward B. Lindeman, *Alternatives for Washington, Pathways to 1985* (Olympia, Wash.: Office of Program Planning and Fiscal Management, 1975), p. 23.

26. William N. Rice, *Agenda for the Eighties: The Forces Shaping Washington's Future*, Vol. 2, *State Growth and The Economy* (Olympia: Washington State Research Council, 1980), pp. 16–17.

27. Neal R. Peirce and Jerry Hagstrom, *The Book of America: Inside Fifty States Today* (New York: Warner Books, 1984), pp. 834, 848–49.

28. Rice, p. 16.

29. Quoted in Rice, p. 1.

30. Ibid., p. 2.

31. Ibid., p. 3.

32. Ibid. I recall, not long after that, the always adroit Ken Dolbeare telling us in a graduate seminar, "The yuppies are coming, and there's nothing you can do to stop them."

33. Ibid., p. 6.

34. Ibid.

35. Ibid.

36. Ibid. pp. 23–24.

37. Rich Nafziger, "The Washington Economy: Problems and Opportunities" (unpublished house Democrat position paper, Aug. 20, 1984), p. 5.

38. Nafziger, p. 27.

39. *Boeing Arms the Corporate Empire*, p. 1.

40. The journalist Joel Garreau wrote that the Pacific Northwest coastal region was "Ecotopia" and marveled that in this land of environmental concern Boeing workers could build cruise missiles with a straight face; see *The Nine Nations of North America* (Boston: Houghton Mifflin, 1981), pp. 280–82. In his defense, he was writing as President Reagan was engaging in a sustained bout of Cold War saber-rattling. On the other hand, Garreau also erroneously wrote that William E. Boeing "was originally from Seattle" (p. 257). The reader may recall that the company founder was born in Detroit.

41. Irving, p. 330.

42. Boeing Company, *Portfolio of Opportunities*, p. 3.

43. Nafziger, pp. 27–28.

44. Ibid., p. 31.

45. Tim Schreiner, "West: One Bright Spot in Washington," *American Demographics*, Sept. 1986, p. 55.

46. Washington State Economic Development Board, *Washington's Challenges and Opportunities in the Global Economy* (Seattle: 1987), p. ix.

47. Ibid., p. 4. A pair of Republican legislators and a pair of business executives, including one from Boeing, wrote a minority report to the tax section, in which they questioned nearly every conclusion reached by the majority, even the obvious ones, and offered no alternatives. See pp. 61–63.

48. Ibid., p. 10.

49. Ibid., p. 35.

50. Washington State Economic Development Board, *The Washington State Economy: An Assessment of Its Strengths and Weaknesses* (Seattle, 1987), p. 9.

51. O. Casey Corr, "The Dark Side of Growth Troubles Seattle as Problems Also Flourish," *Seattle Post-Intelligencer*, Dec. 5, 1988.

52. Ibid.

53. Ibid.

54. Mike Layton, "It's Time to Weigh the Cost of Promoting Growth," *Seattle Post-Intelligencer*, June 27, 1988.

55. Ibid.

56. Anthony Downs, *Stuck in Traffic: Coping with Peak-hour Traffic Congestion* (Washington, D.C.: Brookings Institution, 1992), p. 2.

57. O. Casey Corr, "A Growing Debate: Business Roundtable Strays from Peirce's Path on Development," *Seattle Times*, Dec. 4, 1989.

58. Surveys and focus groups in the 1980s revealed a problem with the urban village concept, however: not many people wanted to live like that.

59. Corr (1989).

60. "Don't Block the View," *The Economist*, May 27, 1989, p. 30.

61. Cited in Corr (1988).

62. Corr (1988).

63. Jeff Cole, "Off Course: Boeing's Bid to Avoid Swings in Its Business Cycle Falls Short of Hopes," *Wall Street Journal*, Feb. 16, 1993.

64. Pascall, Pedersen, and Conway, p. viii.

65. Ed Penhale, "Managing State Growth Looms As Hot Issue for '90 Legislature," *Seattle Post-Intelligencer*, Jan. 1, 1990.

66. Revised Codes of Washington, 36.70A.010.

67. Tim W. Ferguson, "The Mutually Mixed Blessing of Being Home to Boeing," *Wall Street Journal*, Nov. 13, 1990.

68. Ibid., p. A9.

69. Washington State Growth Strategies Commission, *A Growth Strategy for Washington State* (Seattle: 1990), pp. 10–12.

70. Larry Werner, "Growth Plan for 16 Counties Passes House," *Seattle Post-Intelligencer*, Feb. 16, 1990.

71. Teresa J. Taylor, *What 217 Companies Say About Doing Business in King County* (Seattle: Economic Development Council of Seattle and King County, 1993), p. 5.

72. Dolbeare (1983), p. 38.

73. Ibid., p. 44.

74. Jim Simon, "Defeat of Initiative 547 Didn't End Environmental Issue—Gardner," *Seattle Times*, Dec. 15, 1990.

75. Jim Simon, "Bill to Put Teeth in Growth Law on Road to Approval in Olympia," *Seattle Times*, June 28, 1991.

76. Associated Press, "Gardner Signs, Hails New Law to Beef Up Land-Use Planning," *Seattle Times*, July 17, 1991.

77. Cole.

78. Harriet King, "Seattle Builders Turn to Farms and Forests," *New York Times*, April 11, 1993.

79. *The Economist*, "Crash Landing," Jan. 30, 1993, p. 29.

80. Bill Saporito, "The Best Cities for Business," *Fortune*, Nov. 2, 1992, p. 43.

81. Carol Smith Monkman and Graham Fysh, "Boeing Leaves State to Build New Facility," *Seattle Post-Intelligencer*, Aug. 9, 1986.

82. Metropolitan King County Council, "Special Hearings, Economic Development and Job Growth" (Seattle, 1994), p. 3.

83. Ibid.

84. Ibid., p. 6.

CHAPTER 4 / FULL COURT PRESS

1. However, Bishop eventually appeared to be one of the casualties of the McDonnell Douglas acquisition, getting squeezed out the door in 1998 as company production problems mounted and the stock languished again.

2. Ziegler and van Dalen, p. 104.

3. Eugene Rodgers, *Flying High* (New York: Atlantic Monthly Press, 1996), p. 462.

4. Ibid. p. 191.

5. Mike Brennan, "Union Pressures County on Boeing Expansion Stance," *Everett Herald,* Aug. 6, 1991.

CHAPTER 5 / PAPER AIRPLANES IN THE MARBLE ZOO

1. Neal R. Peirce, *The Pacific States of America: People, Politics, and Power in Five Pacific Basin States* (New York: W. W. Norton, 1972), p. 243.

2. Washington State Economic Development Board, *Washington Works Worldwide: Positioning Ourselves to Compete in the New Global Economy* (Olympia, Wash., 1988), p. 57.

3. Ed Penhale, "Boeing Rejects Tax Reform As Not Any Better," *Seattle Post-Intelligencer,* March 30, 1989.

4. Loyal members of his own party told me as much. Then again, the much more politically savvy Dan Evans also failed at pushing an income tax through.

5. Boeing's support—and the support of the state's other large firms—for the B&O is easily explained. The B&O rate is fairly low for manufacturers, and predicated on gross sales, not profits, making it attractive for high-profit firms such as Boeing. A corporate profits tax, conversely, would sting Boeing more deeply in the many years when its profits are high.

6. Associated Press, "Tax Measure Would Take Bigger Piece from Boeing," *Everett Herald,* June 19, 1991.

7. Bill Richards, "Boeing May Go Elsewhere for New Jets," *Seattle Post-Intelligencer,* Sept. 21, 1991.

8. O. Casey Corr, "Power to Persuade," *Seattle Times,* Feb. 9, 1997.

9. Doug Underwood, "In Olympia, Boeing Can Get Just About What Boeing Wants," *Seattle Times,* April 8, 1987.

10. Ibid.

11. Ibid.

12. Walfred H. Peterson, "Interest Groups and Lobbies in Washington State

Government," in Swanson et al., p. 148; and "Washington: The Impact of Public Disclosure Laws," in Ronald J. Hrebenar and Clive S. Thomas, eds., *Interest Group Politics in the American West* (Salt Lake City: University of Utah Press, 1987), pp. 121–31.

13. Walker, pp. 50–54.

14. See for example, T. M. Sell, *Riding the Milk Wagon: The Effect of Money on the Outcomes of Legislative Campaigns in Washington State, 1974–1982* (Olympia: Washington State Public Disclosure Commission, 1985).

15. Randy Ray and Megan Mardesich, *Perceptions: Corporate Political Involvement in the Washington State Legislature* (Olympia: The Evergreen State College, 1976), p. 9.

16. Lynn, p. 185.

17. Bruce Ramsey, "Boeing Acts to Fend Off Takeover Threat," *Seattle Post-Intelligencer,* July 28, 1987.

18. Lynn, p. 186.

19. Ibid.

20. Ed Penhale and Les Gapay, "Lawmakers Look at Boeing Protection," *Seattle Post-Intelligencer,* August 5, 1987.

21. Les Gapay, "Boeing Has Jumbo Impact on Economy," *Seattle Post-Intelligencer,* January 20, 1987.

22. Penhale (1987).

23. Lynn, p. 186.

24. Penhale (1987).

25. Ibid.

26. See Mary Rothschild, "A Tale of Two Sessions—And the Second Belongs to Boeing," *Seattle Post-Intelligencer,* August 11, 1987. Lynn notes that Pickens sold his shares "at a substantial profit," and that the adventure probably killed Boeing's proposed 7J7 jetliner, since Wall Street was not likely to look kindly on a company whose results were down because its development costs were up (pp. 186–87). It is an interesting conjecture from a number of angles; the 7J7 would have been a technological leap ahead with its quiet, fuel-efficient engines. And if Boeing had decided to build it in the Seattle area, the problems generated by the Paradox of Growth might have come to the forefront much sooner than they did.

27. Mike Layton, "Legislature Can Move Quickly If It Wants To," *Seattle Post-Intelligencer,* Aug. 11, 1987.

28. Rodgers, pp. 310–11.

29. Ray and Mardesich, p. 33.

30. Ibid., p. 9.

31. See Underwood.

32. Rodgers, p. 310.

33. Peirce (1972), p. 243.

34. Mike Layton, "Speaker Joe King Is Determined to Smoke Out Boeing's Lobbyists," *Seattle Post-Intelligencer,* May 29, 1987.

35. Ibid.

CHAPTER 6 / THINGS HAPPEN

1. Eugene Rodgers, *Flying High* (New York: Atlantic Monthly Press, 1996), p. 307.

2. Edward C. Banfield, *Big City Politics* (New York: Random House, 1965), p. 133.

3. Nard Jones, *Seattle* (Garden City, N.Y.: Doubleday, 1972), p. 75.

4. Rodgers, p. 311.

5. Nard Jones, p. 28.

6. Scott Johnson, *The Unpolitics of The Boeing Company: Nondecisionmaking and Annexation in Seattle,* unpublished ms., 1993.

7. Rodgers, p. 308.

8. Ibid., pp. 306–8.

9. Gerald B. Nelson, *Seattle: The Life and Times of an American City* (New York: Alfred A. Knopf, 1977), pp. 47–48.

10. I tried, on several occasions, to talk to somebody with the City of Seattle, anybody, to get their side of the story. Mayor Norm Rice's aides did not think the topic worthy of his time, because he was about to run for governor. Officials in the city's economic development office, who might be expected to care about the city's relations with its largest employer, displayed a great knack for the unerring lateral pass to somebody else who did not want to touch the subject.

11. Morda Slauson, *Renton: From Coal to Jets* (Renton, Wash.: Renton Historical Society, 1976), pp. 169–70.

12. Ibid.

13. Associated Press, "The Boeington Blues," *Everett Herald,* Nov. 4, 1990.

14. Kathy Hall, "Boeing to Expand Renton Plant," *Valley Daily News,* March 14, 1989.

15. Tina Hilding, "Panel Studies Boeing Plant Noise," *Valley Daily News,* Nov. 20, 1990.

16. Kathy Hall, "Boeing Agrees to Price for Renton Expansion," *Valley Daily News,* Nov. 14, 1989.

17. Kathy Hall, "Concerns Raised About Boeing Plant," *Valley Daily News*, April 19, 1989.

18. Tina Hilding, "Boeing Noise Raises Voices," *Valley Daily News*, June 6, 1989.

19. Kathy Hall, "Neighbors' Fears Kill Jet-engine Test Plans," *Valley Daily News*, May 28, 1989.

20. Kathy Hall, "City Moves to Muffle Boeing Expansion," *Valley Daily News*, Feb. 23, 1990.

21. Kathy Hall, "Renton Backs Off from Accord on Boeing Noise Mitigation," *Valley Daily News*, March 13, 1990.

22. Kathy Hall, "Expanding Boeing Wants to Be Neighborly," *Valley Daily News*, Sept. 21, 1989.

23. Tina Hilding, "Webb to Fight Till Money Runs Out," *Valley Daily News*, June 20, 1990.

24. Kathy Hall, "Boeing Scales Back Renton Expansion," *Valley Daily News*, April 17, 1990.

25. Kathy Hall, "Boeing Plan Changes Crimp Renton Budget," *Valley Daily News*, April 19, 1990.

26. Associated Press, "The Boeington Blues," op. cit.

27. "Old Jim Nelsen Had a Farm, But Boeing's Got It Now," *Site Selection*, December 1990.

28. Lynn, pp. 84–85.

29. Ibid., pp. 91–92.

30. Irving, pp. 232–33.

31. Ibid. Lynn calls this a "mawkish" view, but I think it has some merit.

32. Rodgers, p. 249.

33. Lynn, pp. 92–93.

34. Serling, p. 287.

35. "Business Watch," *Everett Herald* archives, Nov. 17, 1992, not published.

36. Irving, p. 234.

37. Mike Brennan, "A Bigger Boeing," *Everett Herald*, March 17, 1991.

38. Dale Folkerts, "Boeing Sued for Housing," *Everett Herald*, Aug. 21, 1991.

39. Mike Brennan and Eric Stevick, "County to Drop Appeal of Boeing Plans," *Everett Herald*, Aug. 8, 1991.

40. Associated Press, "Boeing Growth Could Fly Away," *Everett Herald*, Sept. 21, 1991.

41. Associated Press, "Denver Group Hopes to Attract Boeing Business," *Everett Herald*, Sept. 21, 1991.

42. Ken Hunt, "State Eyes Boeing Cutbacks," *Everett Herald*, Feb. 19, 1993.

43. Associated Press, "Expansion of Everett Aircraft Plant Complete," *Everett Herald*, Oct. 5, 1993.

44. Jim Haley, "Everett Asks Commitment from Boeing," *Everett Herald*, Sept. 9, 1993.

45. Bob Wodnik, "Boeing Accepts County Land Offer," *Everett Herald*, March 9, 1994.

46. Bob Wodnik, "Standing at the Brink of a New Era," *Everett Herald*, Jan. 17, 1993.

CHAPTER 7 / CALLING IN THE CAVALRY

1. Testimony before the Metropolitan King County Council, Jan. 21, 1994; see Metropolitan King County Council, "Special Hearings, Economic Development and Job Growth" (Seattle: 1994), p. 5.

2. Ibid., p. 6.

3. Associated Press, "Boeing Complaints on 777 Job Prompt Change in Regulations," *Everett Herald*, Sept. 9, 1993.

4. Eric Stevick, "Permit Grant Boon for Boeing," *Everett Herald*, Aug. 17, 1994.

5. Richard Stanley Davis, "Doing Less with Less," *Washington CEO*, January 1994, p. 41.

6. Washington State Department of Community, Trade, and Economic Development, *Integrating SEPA and GMA: The Promise* (Olympia, 1994), p. 1.

7. Ken Hunt, "State Eyes Boeing Cutbacks," *Everett Herald*, Feb. 19, 1993.

8. Ibid.

9. David Schaefer, "Boeing Pushes for Land-Use Changes," *Seattle Times*, March 1, 1993.

10. Ibid.

11. Ibid.

12. Jeff Mize, "Speaker: Growth Law Surprised State Voters," *Vancouver Columbian*, June 26, 1996.

13. John Rindlaub, Washington Roundtable press release, PR Newswire, Feb. 9, 1995.

14. Peter Neurath, "Legislature Limits Growth Management Review Boards," *Puget Sound Business Journal*, March 22, 1996, p. 6.

15. Glenn R. Pascall, "Let's Find Long-Term Cures for Growing Pains," *Puget Sound Business Journal*, January 2, 1998, p. 39.

CHAPTER 8 / SOFT LANDING

1. The Fourth Law, *Everyone favors economic competition, except when it applies to them,* is not completely relevant to this example. Support for growth management, while economic in nature, did not really involve firms competing for resources with Boeing.

2. Peter Neurath, "Developers Applaud Changes in Growth Management Act," *Puget Sound Business Journal,* May 19, 1995, p. 18.

3. Randy Blair, "Hurdles to Achieving Growth Management Act Goals," *Puget Sound Business Journal,* Nov. 22, 1996, p. 1.

4. Ibid.

5. *The Economist,* "Cities and Growth," June 20, 1998, p. 33.

6. See, for example, Elkin, p. 34.

7. Douglass North, speech at the University of Washington, June 6, 1994.

8. Ibid.

9. Kathie Anderson, "New Jumbo Jet Could Fly Away for Production," *Everett Herald,* Jan. 29, 1993.

10. "Boeing Chairman Traces the Company's California Roots toward a World Vision," company press release, PR Newswire, March 18, 1997.

11. Harrigan, pp. 197–99.

12. Justin Martin, "Cashing In on Relocation Battles," *Fortune,* Sept. 18, 1995, p. 32.

13. *The Economist,* Oct. 3, 1992, p. 29.

14. *The Economist,* Aug. 14, 1993, p. 23.

15. Elkin, p. 33.

16. Robert C. Grady attributes this idea to Robert Reich, Lester Thurow, and Charles Lindblom, among others; see "Reindustrialization, Liberal Democracy, and Corporatist Representation," *Political Science Quarterly,* Fall 1986, pp. 416–23.

17. Stanley Rothman, "The Decline of Bourgeois America," *Society,* January–February 1996, p. 9.

18. See Robert B. Reich, *The Next American Frontier* (New York: Times Books, 1983).

19. Grady, p. 426.

20. Fascinating notions such as QWERTY economics notwithstanding; see Paul Krugman, *Peddling Prosperity: Economic Sense and Nonsense in the Age of Diminished Expectations* (New York: W. W. Norton, 1994), pp. 221–44. Even given an idea such as QWERTY, named for the inefficient keyboard that persists over the far superior Dvorak keyboard, the market can be expected to make nearly optimal decisions more often than not.

21. Moynihan, pp. 19–20.

22. DeLeon, pp. 54–55.

23. Leone, pp. 129–30, 181.

24. Stephen L. Jackstadt and Dwight R. Lee, "Economic Sustainability: The Sad Case of Alaska," *Society,* March–April 1995, p. 52.

25. Ibid., p. 53.

26. *The Federalist,* No. 10.

EPILOGUE

1. David Jacobs, "Corporate Economic Power and the State: A Longitudinal Assessment of Two Explanations," *American Journal of Sociology,* Jan. 1988, p. 852.

2. Charles Edward Lindblom, *Politics and Markets: The World's Political Economic Systems* (New York: Basic Books, 1977), p. 5.

3. Ibid., p. 175.

4. Herbert Kaufman and Victor Jones, "The Mystery of Power," in Aiken and Mott, pp. 233–41.

5. As noted above, Larry Bishop, who wooed securities analysts for the company, also got the axe, as did a number of other mid- and upper-level managers from both Boeing and McDonnell Douglas.

6. Melanie F. Gibbs, "Washington," *National Real Estate Investor,* June 1996, p. 132.

7. I kept envisioning either a lot of people on somebody's porch, or neighbors yelling at each other from across the street, "Hey, what about this growth?"

8. Eric Pryne, "Growth: Enough Already? What If We Close the Door?" *Seattle Times,* Nov. 22, 1998.

9. Pascall, p. 39.

10. Mike Lindblom, "We're Wealthier, But Many Can't Afford a House," *Seattle Times* on-line edition, Sept. 10, 1999, seattletimes.com.

11. Ibid.

12. David Heath, "Software Payrolls Surpass Aerospace As Stock Options Cause Momentous Shift in Puget Sound Area," *Seattle Times* on-line edition, Aug. 22, 1999, seattletimes.com

13. In August 1998, Boeing talked about adding a 737 production line in Long Beach, California, at its newly acquired Douglas Aircraft plant. But the Renton-based 737 line eventually sorted out its production problems, and by December the company had dropped the idea.

14. Washington Roundtable, *Principles for Prosperity: How Washington's Business*

Climate Compares. How Washington Must Change to Compete (Seattle: January 1995), p. 3.

15. Ibid., pp. 3, 5. A member firm, US West, already was calling for local telephone deregulation despite the apparent lack of viable options for most residential customers.

16. Ibid., p. 4.

17. Washington Roundtable, *Preparing for Washington's High-Tech Future* (Seattle: July 1996), p. 5.

18. Rosabeth Moss Kanter, *World Class: Thriving Locally in the Global Economy* (New York: Simon and Schuster, 1995), p. 362. Actually, Seattle and Washington State have attracted a fair amount of outside investment, from such firms as Nintendo, Kyocera, Mitsubishi, Rhone-Poulenc, and Atlas Copco. Kanter apparently set out to find out what made some cities thrive. Although Seattle was thriving, it did not fit her model. Rather than figuring out why, she seems simply to have dismissed it.

19. Brian O'Reilly, "The War Against Growth Heats Up," *Fortune*, Dec. 5, 1988, p. 119. O'Reilly noted that the issue was at that time already sprouting in New York, Virginia, and North Carolina as well.

20. Paula Johnson, "Growth Control Battles Continue," *Colorado Business Magazine*, March 1997, p. 16.

21. Richard Morrill, "Growth Can Be Controlled, But At What Cost?" *Seattle Times*, July 14, 1998.

22. Ibid. Moreover, Morrill called the question of whether growth pays for itself "silly." "Most growth pays for itself over the long run because it provides jobs or shelter, regardless of who pays up front; otherwise, cities and towns couldn't and wouldn't exist."

23. Mike Dobbins and Peggy Dobbins, "Sprawl Things Considered," *American City and County*, Sept. 1997, p. 18.

24. Gayla Smutny, "Legislative Support for Growth Management in the Rocky Mountains: An Exploration of Attitudes in Idaho," *Journal of the American Planning Association*, Summer 1998, pp. 311–23. Many Idahoans now say "don't Californicate Idaho" (p. 317), and yet for at least a decade the state has actively recruited California firms to relocate.

25. Noam Neusner, "Flush with Cash, States Vie for Riches of High-tech Jobs," *Seattle Times* on-line edition, Aug. 13, 1999, seattletimes.com

26. And its more stringent cousin, BANANA: Build Absolutely Nothing Anywhere Near Anyone.

27. Christopher Leo, Mary Ann Beavis, Andrew Carver, and Robyne Turner, "Is

Urban Sprawl Back on the Political Agenda? Local Growth Control, Regional Growth Management, and Politics," *Urban Affairs Review,* November 1998, pp. 179–211.

28. Ibid. Leo questions whether the growth boundary was the source of rising prices there, however, noting that some cities without growth controls had bigger housing price gains than did Portland.

29. Debby Hopkins, speech, PR Newswire, Dec. 8, 1999.

30. Kery Murakami, "Is Federal Way Doing Its Share to Handle Growth?" *Seattle Times* on-line edition, Aug. 3, 1999, seattletimes.com

31. See Benjamin R. Barber, *Strong Democracy: Participatory Politics for a New Age* (Berkeley: University of California Press, 1984).

32. This is not to argue for unfettered capitalism, which surely would self-destruct if left to its own devices. But here's the deal: liberal, capitalist democracy is a miserable socioeconomic system. Everything else is worse.

33. I like to think of myself as a militant moderate, aggressively seeking and supporting balance, fairness, and compromise.

Bibliography

ARTICLES

Aberdeen Daily World. "W. E. Boeing, Plane Company Founder, Called." September 29, 1956.

Alperovitz, Gar, and Jeff Faux. "Think Again: What We Need Is More Government, Not Less." *Washington Post,* National Weekly Edition, Oct. 22, 1984.

Anderson, Kathie. "New Jumbo Jet Could Fly Away for Production." *Everett Herald,* Jan. 29, 1993.

Associated Press. "The Boeington Blues." *Everett Herald,* Nov. 4, 1990.

_____. "Tax Measure Would Take Bigger Piece from Boeing." *Everett Herald,* June 19, 1991.

_____. "Gardner Signs, Hails New Law to Beef Up Land-Use Planning." *Seattle Times,* July 17, 1991.

_____. "Boeing Growth Could Fly Away." *Everett Herald,* Sept. 21, 1991.

_____. "Denver Group Hopes To Attract Boeing Business." *Everett Herald,* Sept. 21, 1991.

_____. "Boeing Complaints On 777 Job Prompt Change in Regulations." *Everett Herald,* Sept. 9, 1993.

_____. "Expansion of Everett Aircraft Plant Complete." *Everett Herald,* Oct. 5, 1993.

Bachrach, Peter, and Morton S. Baratz, "Decisions and Nondecisions: An Analytical Framework," in Aiken and Mott, pp. 308–20.

_____. "Two Faces of Power," in Nivola and Rosenbloom, pp. 142–51.

Blair, Randy. "Hurdles to Achieving Growth Management Act Goals." *Puget Sound Business Journal,* Nov. 22, 1996.

Bone, Hugh A. "The Political Setting," in Swanson et al., pp. 1–18.

Boswell, Sharon, and Lorraine McConaghy, "Doing The Dirty Work: A Region

Ravaged By Rapid Growth Sounds the Call to Clean the Water, Clear the Air."
   Seattle Times, Sept. 15, 1996.

Brennan, Mike. "A Bigger Boeing." *Everett Herald,* March 17, 1991.

_____. "Union Pressures County on Boeing Expansion Stance." *Everett Herald,* Aug.
   6, 1991.

_____ and Eric Stevick. "County to Drop Appeal of Boeing Plans." *Everett Herald,*
   Aug. 8, 1991.

Clelland, Donald A., and William H. Form. "Economic Dominants and Community Power: A Comparative Analysis," in Aiken and Mott, pp. 67–77.

Cole, Jeff. "Off Course: Boeing's Bid to Avoid Swings in Its Business Cycle Falls
   Short of Hopes." *Wall Street Journal,* Feb. 16, 1993.

Corr, O. Casey. "The Dark Side Of Growth Troubles Seattle As Problems Also
   Flourish." *Seattle Post-Intelligencer,* Dec. 5, 1988.

_____. "A Growing Debate, Business Roundtable Strays from Peirce's Path on
   Development." *Seattle Times,* Dec. 4, 1989.

_____. "Power to Persuade." *Seattle Times,* Feb. 9, 1997.

Dahl, Robert A. "From Oligarchy to Pluralism: The Patricians and the Entrepreneurs," in Aiken and Mott, pp. 31–45.

_____. "The Concept of Power," pp. 202–203, in Morehouse, p. 103.

_____. "Who Governs," in Hawley and Wirt, pp. 87–107.

_____. "Rethinking *Who Governs?*: New Haven Revisited," in *Waste* (1986), pp.
   179–96.

Davis, Richard Stanley. "Doing Less with Less." *Washington CEO,* January 1994,
   pp. 40–42.

Dobbins, Mike, and Peggy Dobbins. "Sprawl Things Considered: Controlling
   Growth." *American City & County,* September 1997, p. 18.

Domhoff, G. William. "The Growth Machine and the Power Elite: A Challenge to
   Pluralists and Marxists Alike," in *Waste* (1986), pp. 53–75.

Dowding, Keith, Patrick Dunleavy, Desmond King, and Helen Margetts. "Rational
   Choice and Community Power Structures." *Political Studies,* June 1995, pp.
   265–77.

Dye, Thomas R. "Community Power and Public Policy," in *Waste* (1986), pp. 29–51.

_____, and L. Harmon Ziegler, "Elites in States and Communities," in Leach and
   O'Rourke, pp. 75–87.

The Economist, "Don't Block the View." May 27, 1989.

_____. "Et in Cascadia, Ego." Feb. 29, 1992.

_____. "When Big Pips Squeak." Oct. 3, 1992.

_____. "Crash Landing." Jan. 30, 1993.

_____. "Money to Burn." Aug. 14, 1993.

_____. "Cities And Growth: Paradise Overrun." June 20, 1998.

Ferguson, Tim W. "The Mutually Mixed Blessing of Being Home to Boeing." *Wall Street Journal*, Nov. 13, 1990.

Folkerts, Dale. "Boeing Sued for Housing." *Everett Herald*, Aug. 21, 1991.

French, Robert Mills. "Economic Change and Community Power Structure: Transition in Cornucopia," in Aiken and Mott, pp. 180–89.

Gapay, Les. "Boeing Has Jumbo Impact on Economy." *Seattle Post-Intelligencer*, Jan. 20, 1987.

Gibbs, Melanie F. "Washington." *National Real Estate Investor*, June 1996, pp. 132–33.

Grady, Robert C. "Reindustrialization, Liberal Democracy and Corporatist Representation." *Political Science Quarterly*, Fall 1986, pp. 415–32.

Gustison, Mrs. Sutton. "The Boeing Story." *Pacific Northwest Quarterly*, April 1954, pp. 41–46.

Haley, Jim. "Everett Asks Commitment from Boeing." *Everett Herald*, Sept. 9, 1993.

Hall, Kathy. "Boeing to Expand Renton Plant." *Valley Daily News*, March 14, 1989.

_____. "Concerns Raised About Boeing Plant." *Valley Daily News*, April 19, 1989.

_____. "Neighbors' Fears Kill Jet-Engine Test Plans." *Valley Daily News*, May 28, 1989.

_____. "Boeing Agrees to Price for Renton Expansion." *Valley Daily News*, Nov. 14, 1989.

_____. "Expanding Boeing Wants to Be Neighborly." *Valley Daily News*, Sept. 21, 1989.

_____. "City Moves to Muffle Boeing Expansion." *Valley Daily News*, Feb. 23, 1990.

_____. "Renton Backs Off from Accord on Boeing Noise Mitigation." *Valley Daily News*, March 13, 1990.

_____. "Boeing Scales Back Renton Expansion." *Valley Daily News*, April 17, 1990, p. A1.

_____. "Boeing Plan Changes Crimp Renton Budget." *Valley Daily News*, April 19, 1990.

Heath, David. "Software Payrolls Surpass Aerospace As Stock Options Cause Momentous Shift in Puget Sound Area." *Seattle Times* on-line edition, Aug. 22, 1999, seattletimes.com.

Hilding, Tina. "Boeing Noise Raises Voices." *Valley Daily News*, June 6, 1989.

_____. "Webb to Fight Till Money Runs Out." *Valley Daily News*, June 20, 1990.

_____. "Panel Studies Boeing Plant Noise." *Valley Daily News*, Nov. 20, 1990.

Hrebenar, Ronald J. "Interest Group Politics in the American West: A Comparative Perspective," in Hrebenar and Thomas, pp. 3–11 .

Hunt, Ken. "State Eyes Boeing Cutbacks." *Everett Herald*, Feb. 19, 1993.

Jackstadt, Stephen L., and Dwight R. Lee. "Economic Sustainability: The Sad Case of Alaska." *Society,* March–April 1995, pp. 50–54.

Jacobs, David. "Corporate Economic Power and the State: A Longitudinal Assessment of Two Explanations." *American Journal of Sociology,* January 1988, pp. 852–81.

Johnson, Paula. "Growth Control Battles Continue." *Colorado Business Magazine,* March 1997, pp. 16–19.

Kaufman, Herbert, and Victor Jones. "The Mystery of Power," in Aiken and Mott, pp. 233–41.

King, Harriet. "Seattle Builders Turn to Farms and Forests." *New York Times,* April 11, 1993.

Kirkendall, Richard S. "The Boeing Company and the Military-Metropolitan-Industrial Complex, 1945–1953." *Pacific Northwest Quarterly,* October 1994, pp. 137–49.

———. "Two Senators and the Boeing Company." *Columbia,* Winter 1997–98, pp. 38–43.

Layton, Mike. "Speaker Joe King Is Determined to Smoke Out Boeing's Lobbyists." *Seattle Post-Intelligencer,* May 29, 1987.

———. "Legislature Can Move Quickly If It Wants To." *Seattle Post-Intelligencer,* Aug. 11, 1987.

———. "It's Time to Weigh the Cost of Promoting Growth." *Seattle Post-Intelligencer,* June 27, 1988.

Leo, Christopher, Mary Ann Beavis, Andrew Carver, and Robyne Turner. "Is Urban Sprawl Back on the Political Agenda? Local Growth Control, Regional Growth Management, and Politics." *Urban Affairs Review,* November 1998, pp. 179–211.

Lindblom, Mike. "We're Wealthier, But Many Can't Afford a House." *Seattle Times* on-line edition, Sept. 10, 1999, seattletimes.com.

Logan, John E., and Arthur B. Moore, Jr. "Better Decision Making in Ecological Disputes," in Sethi, pp. 362–76.

Martin, Justin. "Cashing In on Relocation Battles." *Fortune,* Sept. 18, 1995, p. 32.

Miller, Delbert C. "Industry and Community Power Structures: A Comparative Study of an American and an English City." *American Sociological Review,* February 1958; rpt. in Aiken and Mott, pp. 412–19.

———. "Decision-Making Cliques in Community Power Structures: A Comparative Study of an American and an English City." *American Journal of Sociology,* November 1958; rpt. in Aiken and Mott, pp. 419–30.

Mize, Jeff. "Speaker: Growth Law Surprised State Voters." *Vancouver Columbian,* June 26, 1996.

Monkman, Carol Smith, and Graham Fysh. "Boeing Leaves State to Build New Facility." *Seattle Post-Intelligencer,* Aug. 9, 1986.

Morrill, Richard. "Growth Can Be Controlled, But At What Cost?" *Seattle Times,* July 14, 1998.

Mott, Paul E. "Power, Authority, and Influence," in Aiken and Mott, pp. 3–16.

Moynihan, Daniel P. "The Social Responsibility of Business," in Daniel P. Moynihan, *Business and Society in Change* (New York: AT&T, 1975), pp. 8–26.

Mullen, William F., and John C. Pierce. "Political Parties," in Swanson et al., pp. 55–73.

Murakami, Kery. "Is Federal Way Doing Its Share to Handle Growth?" *Seattle Times* on-line edition, Aug. 3, 1999, seattletimes.com.

Neurath, Peter. "Developers Applaud Changes in Growth Management Act." *Puget Sound Business Journal,* May 19, 1995.

_____. "Legislature Limits Growth Management Review Boards." *Puget Sound Business Journal,* March 22, 1996.

Neusner, Noam. "Flush with Cash, States Vie for Riches of High-tech Jobs." *Seattle Times* on-line edition, Aug. 13, 1999, seattletimes.com.

"Old Jim Nelsen Had a Farm, But Boeing's Got It Now." *Site Selection,* December 1990.

O'Reilly, Brian. "The War Against Growth Heats Up." *Fortune,* Dec. 5, 1988, p. 119.

Pascall, Glenn R. "Let's Find Long-Term Cures For Growing Pains." *Puget Sound Business Journal,* Jan. 2, 1998.

Penhale, Ed. "Gardner May Call Session for Aug. 10." *Seattle Post-Intelligencer,* July 29, 1987.

_____ and Les Gapay, "Lawmakers Look at Boeing Protection." *Seattle Post-Intelligencer,* Aug. 5, 1987.

_____. "Top Legislators Back Boeing Bill." *Seattle Post-Intelligencer,* Aug. 7, 1987.

_____. "Legislature Likely to Act on Boeing Today." *Seattle Post-Intelligencer,* Aug. 10, 1987.

_____. "Boeing Gets Protection Against Raider, *Seattle Post-Intelligencer,* Aug. 11, 1987.

_____. "Boeing Rejects Tax Reform As Not Any Better." *Seattle Post-Intelligencer,* March 30, 1989.

_____. "Managing State Growth Looms As Hot Issue for '90 Legislature." *Seattle Post-Intelligencer,* Jan. 1, 1990.

Peterson, Walfred H. "Washington: The Impact of Public Disclosure Laws," in Hrebenar and Thomas, pp. 121–31.

_____. "Interest Groups and Lobbies in Washington State Government," in Swanson et al., pp. 141–59.

Pryne, Eric. "Growth Enough Already? What If We Close the Door?" *Seattle Times*,
    Nov. 22, 1998.

Ramsey, Bruce. "Boeing Acts to Fend Off Takeover Threat." *Seattle Post-Intelligencer*,
    July 28, 1987.

Reeves, Belle. "War Production in Washington," in Richards et al., pp. 283–86.

Richards, Bill. "Boeing May Go Elsewhere for New Jets." *Seattle Post-Intelligencer*,
    Sept. 21, 1991.

Rothman, Stanley. "The Decline of Bourgeois America." *Society*, January–February
    1996, pp. 9–16.

Rothschild, Mary. "A Tale of Two Sessions: And the Second Belongs to Boeing."
    Seattle Post-Intelligencer, Aug. 11, 1987.

Saporito, Bill. "The Best Cities for Business." *Fortune*, Nov. 2, 1992, pp. 40–50.

Schaefer, David. "Boeing Pushes for Land-Use Changes." *Seattle Times*, March 1, 1993.

Schreiner, Tim. "West: One Bright Spot in Washington." *American Demographics*,
    September 1986, p. 55.

Schulze, Robert O. "The Role of Economic Dominants in Community Power Struc-
    ture," in Aiken and Mott, pp. 60–67.

Simon, Jim. "Defeat of Initiative 547 Didn't End Environmental Issue—Gardner."
    Seattle Times, Dec. 15, 1990.

_____. "Bill to Put Teeth in Growth Law on Road to Approval in Olympia." *Seattle
    Times*, June 28, 1991.

Smutny, Gayla. "Legislative Support for Growth Management in the Rocky Moun-
    tains: An Exploration of Attitudes in Idaho." *Journal of the American Planning
    Association*, Summer 1998, pp. 311–23.

Starkman, Ernest S. "Imposed Constraints on the Auto Industry: A View from Two
    Perspectives," in Sethi, pp. 328–44.

Stevick, Eric. "Permit Grant Boon for Boeing." *Everett Herald*, Aug. 17, 1994.

Stone, Clarence N. "Power and Social Complexity," in *Waste* (1986), pp. 77–113.

Thomas, Clive, and Ronald J. Hrebenar. "Interest Groups in the States," in Gray et
    al., pp. 123–58.

Underwood, Doug. "In Olympia, Boeing Can Get Just About What Boeing Wants."
    Seattle Times, April 8, 1987.

Walker, Elizabeth. "Interest Groups in Washington State," in Nice et al., pp. 41–63.

Werner, Larry. "Growth Plan for 16 Counties Passes House." *Seattle Post-
    Intelligencer*, Feb. 16, 1990.

Wilson, Cynthia H. "Emperor of the Skies: The Boeings," in Brewster and Buerge,
    pp. 179–86.

Wilson, Graham. "American Business and Politics," in Cigler and Loomis, pp. 221–35.

Wodnik, Bob. "Standing at the Brink of a New Era." *Everett Herald,* Jan. 17, 1993.

_____. "Boeing Accepts County Land Offer." *Everett Herald,* March 9, 1994.

Ziegler, L. Harmon, and Henrik van Dalen. "Interest Groups in State Politics," in Jacob and Vines, pp. 95–119.

                                    BOOKS

Aiken, Michael T., and Paul E. Mott, eds. *The Structure of Community Power.* New York: Random House, 1970.

Allison, Graham T. *Essence of Decision: Explaining the Cuban Missile Crisis.* Boston: Little, Brown, 1971.

Banfield, Edward C. *Big City Politics.* New York: Random House, 1965.

Barber, Benjamin R. *Strong Democracy: Participatory Politics for a New Age.* Berkeley: University of California Press, 1984.

Bauer, E. E. *Boeing in Peace and War.* Enumclaw, Wash.: TABA Publishing, 1990.

Berner, Richard C. *Seattle 1900–1920: From Boomtown and Urban Turbulence to Restoration.* Seattle: Charles Press, 1991.

_____. *Seattle 1921–1940: From Boom to Bust.* Seattle: Charles Press, 1992.

Brewster, David, and David Buerge. *Washingtonians: A Biographical Portrait of the State.* Seattle: Sasquatch Books, 1988.

Buchholz, Todd G. *New Ideas from Dead Economists: An Introduction to Modern Economic Thought.* New York: Penguin Books, 1990.

Chasan, Daniel Jack. *The Water Link: A History of Puget Sound as a Resource.* Seattle: Washington Sea Grant Program, 1981.

_____ and Heather Doran Barbieri. *Seattle: World Class City.* Seattle: Windsor Publications, 1991.

Cigler, Allan J., and Burdett A. Loomis. *Interest Group Politics.* Washington, D.C.: Congressional Quarterly Press, 1986.

Cohn, Edwin J., Jr. *Industry in the Pacific Northwest and the Location Theory.* New York: King's Crown Press, 1954.

Collins, James C., and Jerry I. Porras. *Built to Last: Successful Habits of Visionary Companies.* New York: Harper Collins, 1997.

Crenson, Matthew A. *The Un-politics of Air Pollution: A Study of Non-decisionmaking in the Cities.* Baltimore: Johns Hopkins University Press, 1971.

Cunningham, William Glenn. *The Aircraft Industry: A Study in Industrial Location.* Los Angeles: Lorin L. Morrison, 1951.

Dahl, Robert Alan. *Who Governs? Democracy and Power in an American City.* New Haven: Yale University Press, 1961.

DeLeon, Richard Edward. *Left Coast City: Progressive Politics in San Francisco, 1975–1991.* Lawrence: University Press of Kansas, 1992.

Downs, Anthony. *Stuck in Traffic: Coping with Peak-Hour Traffic Congestion.* Washington, D.C.: Brookings Institution, 1992.

Easton, David. *A Framework for Political Analysis.* Englewood Cliffs, N.J.: Prentice-Hall, 1965.

Eisinger, Peter K. *The Rise of the Entrepreneurial State.* Madison: University of Wisconsin Press, 1988.

Elkin, Stanley L. *City and Regime in the American Republic.* Chicago: University of Chicago Press, 1987.

Ficken, Robert E., and Charles P. LeWarne. *Washington: A Centennial History.* Seattle: University of Washington Press, 1989.

Garreau, Joel. *The Nine Nations of North America.* Boston: Houghton Mifflin, 1981.

Gaventa, John. *Power and Powerlessness: Quiescence and Rebellion in an Appalachian Valley.* Urbana: University of Illinois Press, 1980.

Gray, Virginia, Herbert Jacob, and Robert B. Albritton. *Politics in the American States.* Glenview, Ill.: Scott, Foresman, 1990.

Habermas, Jürgen. *Legitimation Crisis.* Trans. Thomas McCarthy. New York: Beacon Press, 1990.

Hamilton, Alexander, James Madison, and John Jay. *The Federalist.* New York: Random House, 1937.

Harrigan, John J. *Political Change in the Metropolis.* New York: Harper Collins, 1993.

Hawley, Willis D., and Frederick M. Wirt, eds. *The Search for Community Power.* Englewood Cliffs, N.J.: Prentice Hall, 1974.

Hrebenar, Ronald J., and Clive Thomas, eds. *Interest Group Politics in the American West.* Salt Lake City: University of Utah Press, 1987.

Hunter, Floyd. *Community Power Structure: A Study of Decision Makers.* Chapel Hill: University of North Carolina Press, 1953.

Irving, Clive. *Wide Body: The Triumph of the 747.* New York: William Morrow and Co., 1993.

Jacob, Herbert, and Kenneth N. Vines, eds. *Politics in the American States.* Boston: Little, Brown, 1976.

Jacobs, Jane. *Cities and the Wealth of Nations.* New York: Random House, 1984.

Jones, Bryan D., and Lynn W. Bachelor. *The Sustaining Hand: Community Leadership and Corporate Power.* Lawrence: University Press of Kansas, 1993.

Jones, Nard. *Seattle.* Garden City, N.Y.: Doubleday, 1972.

Kanter, Rosabeth Moss. *World Class: Thriving Locally in the Global Economy.* New York: Simon & Schuster, 1995.

Katznelson, Ira. *City Trenches: Urban Politics and the Patterning of Class in the United States*. New York: Pantheon Books, 1981.

Krugman, Paul R. *Peddling Prosperity: Economic Sense and Nonsense in the Age of Diminishing Expectations*. New York: W. W. Norton, 1994.

Lasswell, Harold Dwight, and Abraham Kaplan. *Power and Society: A Framework for Political Inquiry*. New Haven: Yale University Press, 1950.

Leach, Richard H., and Timothy G. O'Rourke. *Dimensions of State and Urban Policy Making*. New York: MacMillan, 1975.

Leone, Robert A. *Who Profits: Winners, Losers, and Government Regulation*. New York: Basic Books, 1986.

Lindblom, Charles Edward. *Politics and Markets: The World's Political Economic Systems*. New York: Basic Books, 1977.

Logan, John R., and Harvey L. Molotch. *Urban Fortunes: The Political Economy of Place*. Berkeley: University of California Press, 1987.

Lotchin, Roger W. *Fortress California, 1910–1961*. New York: Oxford University Press, 1992.

Lowi, Theodore J. *The End of Liberalism: The Second Republic of the United States*. New York: W. W. Norton, 1979.

Lukes, Steven. *Power: A Radical View*. London: MacMillan, 1974.

Lynn, Matthew. *Birds of Prey: Boeing vs. Airbus, a Battle for the Skies*. New York: Four Walls Eight Windows, 1997.

Mansfield, Harold. *Vision: The Story of Boeing*. New York: Popular Press, 1966.

McCann, John. *Blood in the Water: A History of District Lodge 751, International Association of Machinists and Aerospace Workers*. Seattle: District Lodge 751 (in association with the Labor Education and Research Center, The Evergreen State College), 1989.

McDonald, Norbert. *Distant Neighbors: A Comparative History of Seattle and Vancouver*. Lincoln: University of Nebraska Press, 1987.

Mollenkopf, John H. *The Contested City*. Princeton, N.J.: Princeton University Press, 1983.

Morehouse, Sarah McCally. *State Politics, Parties, and Policy*. New York: Holt, Rinehart and Winston, 1981.

Morgan, Murray. *Skid Road: An Informal Portrait of Seattle*. Sausalito, Calif.: Comstock Editions, 1978.

Moynihan, Daniel P. *Business and Society in Change*. New York: AT&T, 1975.

Nash, Gerald D. *The American West in the Twentieth Century: A Short History of an Urban Oasis*. Englewood Cliffs, N.J.: Prentice-Hall, 1973.

_____. *The American West Transformed: The Impact of the Second World War*. Bloomington: Indiana University Press, 1985.

_____. *World War II and the West: Reshaping the Economy.* Lincoln: University of Nebraska Press, 1990.

Nelson, Gerald B. *Seattle: The Life and Times of an American City.* New York: Alfred A. Knopf, 1977.

Newhouse, John. *The Sporty Game.* New York: Alfred A. Knopf, 1982.

Nice, David C., John C. Pierce, and Charles H. Sheldon, eds., *Government and Politics in the Evergreen State.* Pullman: Washington State University Press, 1992.

Nivola, Pietro S., and David H. Rosenbloom. *Classic Readings in American Politics.* New York: St. Martin's Press, 1986.

O'Connor, James. *The Fiscal Crisis of the State.* New York: St. Martin's Press, 1973.

Ogden, Daniel M., Jr., and Hugh A. Bone *Washington Politics.* New York: New York University Press, 1960.

Peirce, Neal R. *The Pacific States of America: People, Politics, and Power in Five Pacific Basin States.* New York: W. W. Norton, 1972.

_____. *Citistates: How Urban America Can Prosper in a Competitive World.* Washington, D.C.: Seven Locks Press, 1993.

_____, and Jerry Hagstrom. *The Book of America: Inside Fifty States Today.* New York: Warner Books, 1984.

Peterson, Paul E. *City Limits.* Chicago: University of Chicago Press, 1981.

Reich, Robert B. *The Next American Frontier.* New York: Times Books, 1983.

Reisman, David. *The Lonely Crowd.* New Haven: Yale University Press, 1950.

Richards, Kent D., Raymond A. Smith, Burton J. Williams, eds. *Washington: Readings in the History of the Evergreen State.* Lawrence, Kans.: Coronado Press, 1975.

Rodgers, Eugene. *Flying High: The Story of Boeing and the Rise of the Jetliner Industry.* New York: Atlantic Monthly Press, 1996.

Sabbagh, Karl. *Twenty-First-Century Jet: The Making and Marketing of the Boeing 777.* New York: Scribner, 1996.

Sale, Roger. *Seattle, Past to Present.* Seattle: University of Washington Press, 1976.

Schattschneider, E. E. *The Semi-Sovereign People: A Realist's View of Democracy in America.* New York: Holt, Rinehart and Winston, 1960.

Serling, Robert J. *Legend and Legacy: The Story of Boeing and Its People.* New York: St. Martin's Press, 1992.

Sethi, S. Prakash, ed. *The Unstable Ground: Corporate Social Policy in a Dynamic Society.* Los Angeles: Melville Publishing, 1974.

Slauson, Morda C. *Renton: From Coal to Jets.* Renton, Wash.: Renton Historical Society, 1976.

Swanson, Thor, William F. Mullen, John C. Pierce, and Charles H. Sheldon, eds. *Political Life in Washington: Governing the Evergreen State.* Pullman, Wash.: Washington State University Press, 1985.

Warren, James R. *A Century of Seattle's Business.* Bellevue, Wash.: Vernon Publications, 1989.

Waste, Robert J., ed. *Community Power: Directions for Further Research.* Beverly Hills: Sage Publications, 1986.

_____. *Power and Pluralism in American Cities.* New York: Greenwood Press, 1987.

Wilson, Graham K. *Business and Politics: A Comparative Introduction.* Chatham, N.J.: Chatham House Publishers, 1990.

MISCELLANEOUS

Sources not otherwise credited come from interviews conducted by the author or from speeches at which the author was present.

"Boeing Chairman Traces the Company's California Roots toward a World Vision." Company press release, PR Newswire, March 18, 1997.

Boeing Company. *Portfolio of Opportunities: A Study Of Some Specific Programs to Provide Economic Assistance to the West Coast.* Seattle: Boeing, 1975.

Business Executives' Research Committee. *The Impact of World War II Subcontracting by the Boeing Airplane Company upon Pacific Northwest Manufacturing.* Seattle: University of Washington, January 1995.

"Business Watch." *Everett Herald* archives, Nov. 17, 1992, not published.

Dolbeare, Kenneth M. *Economic Development and Jobs in Washington: A Citizen's Guide.* Olympia, Wash.: The Evergreen State College, 1983.

_____. *The Evolution of the Public Sector in Washington State.* Olympia: The Evergreen State College, 1988.

Hopkins, Debby. Speech, PR Newswire, Dec. 8, 1999.

Johnson, Scott. *The Unpolitics of The Boeing Company: Nondecisionmaking and Annexation in Seattle.* Unpublished ms., 1993.

Lindeman, Edward B., chairman, Alternatives for Washington Statewide Citizen Task Force. *Alternatives for Washington, Pathways to 1985.* Olympia: Office of Program Planning and Fiscal Management, May 1975.

Metropolitan King County Council. "Special Hearings, Economic Development and Job Growth." Seattle: 1994.

Nafziger, Rich. "The Washington Economy: Problems and Opportunities." Unpublished House Democrat position paper, Aug. 20, 1984.

North, Douglass. Speech at the University of Washington, June 6, 1994.

Office of Program Planning and Fiscal Management. *Alternatives for Washington:*

Pathways to 1985. Alternatives for Washington Statewide Citizen Task Force, May 1975.

Pacific Northwest Research Center. *Boeing Arms the Corporate Empire.* Eugene, Ore.: December 1974.

Pascall, Glenn, Douglas H. Pedersen, and Richard S. Conway, Jr. "The Boeing Company Economic Impact Study." Seattle: Boeing, 1989.

Ray, Randy, and Megan Mardesich. *Perceptions: Corporate Political Involvement in the Washington State Legislature.* Olympia: The Evergreen State College, 1976.

Rice, William N. *Agenda for the Eighties: The Forces Shaping Washington's Future.* Vol. 2, *State Growth and the Economy.* Olympia: Washington State Research Council, 1980.

Rindlaub, John. Washington Roundtable press release, PR Newswire, Feb. 9, 1995.

Sell, T. M. *Riding the Milk Wagon: The Effect of Money on the Outcomes of Legislative Campaigns in Washington State, 1974–1982.* Olympia: Washington State Public Disclosure Commission, 1985.

Taylor, Teresa J. *What 217 Companies Say About Doing Business in King County.* Seattle: Economic Development Council of Seattle and King County, March 1993.

Vander Meulen, Jacob. "West Coast Aircraft Labor and an American Military Industrial Complex, 1935–1941." Working Paper No. 4. Seattle: Center for Labor Studies, University of Washington, 1996.

Washington Roundtable. *Principles for Prosperity: How Washington's Business Climate Compares. How Washington Must Change to Compete.* Seattle: January 1995.

_____. *Preparing for Washington's High-Tech Future.* Seattle: July 1996.

Washington State Department of Community, Trade, and Economic Development. *Integrating SEPA and GMA: The Promise.* Olympia, Wash.: 1994.

Washington State Economic Development Board. *Washington's Challenges and Opportunities in the Global Economy.* Seattle: 1987.

_____. *The Washington State Economy: An Assessment of Its Strengths and Weaknesses.* Prepared for the Board by Dick Conway and Associates. Seattle: 1987

_____. *Washington Works Worldwide: Positioning Ourselves to Compete in the New Global Economy.* Olympia: 1988.

Washington State Growth Strategies Commission. *A Growth Strategy for Washington State.* Seattle: 1990.

Washington State Local Governance Study Commission. *A History of Washington's Local Governments: Final Report.* Volume 1. Olympia: The Commission, Institute of Public Policy, The Evergreen State College, 1988.

Index

Aberdeen, Wash., 13, 19

Airbus, 5, 30, 58, 73, 104, 111, 131n

Alaska, 15, 111

Allen, William, 20, 21, 22, 23, 24, 25, 52, 55, 57, 69

Aluminum, 19, 27

Argus magazine, 27

Association of Washington Businesses, xxiv, 51, 61, 65, 67, 100–101

B-17, 20

Beck, Dave, 22, 29

Beighle, Douglas, 50, 51, 77, 81, 90

Bishop, Larry, 54–55

Boeing, William E., 12–14, 17–19, 52, 78, 79

Boeing Bust, ix, 25–26, 28, 39, 117, 134–35n

Bone, Senator Homer, 19, 25

Brewster, David, 27

Bundy, Emory, 39–40

California, 10, 14, 16, 21, 22, 86, 108–9, 120, 145n

Clifford, Chris, 83–84, 103

Coffey, Forrest G. ("Bud"), 53, 54, 55, 56, 57, 61, 64, 65, 68, 69–73, 77, 84, 93, 116

Cohn, Edwin J. Jr., 15, 37

Condit, Phil, 26, 29, 51, 52, 61, 97, 100

Contributions, 53–54, 65; campaign, 64–66

Conway, Dick, 27, 30, 43, 49

Covington, Jay, 74, 76, 79, 80, 82, 83, 84

Defense Plant Corporation, 18

DeLeon, Richard, xix–xx, 110

Depression, the, 26, 34

Desimone, Guiseppe, 17

Dolbeare, Kenneth, 3, 33, 42, 47–48, 130n

Domhoff, G. William, xix

Duwamish Basin, 7, 13, 16, 17, 74, 77, 95

Dye, Thomas R., xix

Easton, David, xxvii

Elazar, Daniel, 35

Elite theory, xvii–xx, xxi, xxiii–xxiv, 102–3, 126n

Evans, Governor Dan, 60–61, 65, 66, 67, 68, 70, 107–8

Everett, 3, 4, 7–8, 19, 46, 50, 72, 76, 77, 78, 83, 85–94, 98, 112

Funders Group, 99–100

Gardner, Governor Booth, 48, 50, 62–63, 67, 85, 106

Gay, Andre ("Andy"), 51, 61, 95–96, 98

Grant, Gary, 64

Grimm, Dan, 32, 64, 69, 71, 72

Growth coalition, xviii, xi, xix–xx, xxii–xxiii, xxv, 10, 15, 125n

Growth management: efforts outside Washington State, 120–21

Growth Management Act, xi, 7, 45–48, 74, 88, 91, 92, 95, 98–99, 100–101, 107, 118

Habermas, Jurgen, 10, 129n

Hayden, John, 70, 71, 77

Hopkins, Deborah ("Debby"), 121–22

Horn, James, 55–56, 60

Housing, 44, 49, 88, 89, 107, 117

Integrated Aircraft Systems Laboratory, 77

Interest groups, xxiii

International Association of Machinists and Aerospace Workers, 17, 22, 23, 57–59, 67–69, 130n

Jacobs, Jane, 31, 134–35n

Kanter, Rosabeth Moss, 119, 146n

Kinch, Peter 67–68, 78, 88, 90–92

Lanham, Linda, 59, 68, 70

Leone, Robert, xxviii, 110

Levy, Douglas, 72

Lewis, Terrence ("Terry"), 70, 75–77, 93–94

Lindblom, Charles, xv, 110, 112, 115

Longacres, 83–84

Lowry, Governor Mike, 5, 97, 100

Machinists. See International Association of Machinists and Aerospace Workers

Madison, James, xvi, 112

Makin, Rob, 61–62, 65, 67, 71–73, 97, 116

Marxist theory, xvii–xviii, xx, xxviii, 102, 114

McDonnell Douglas, 5, 6, 24, 30, 66, 108, 116

Metro, 34, 81

Mississippi, 119

Moynihan, Daniel Patrick, 10, 110, 129n

Muckleshoot Indian Tribe, 85

Museum of Flight (Seattle), 53

Nafziger, Richard ("Rich"), 41–42

North, Douglass, 108

Oregon, 10, 27, 36, 121

Pacific Aero Products, 13

Pacific Northwest Research Center, 41–42

Paradox of Growth, 8–10, 44, 50, 73, 74, 77–79, 88, 91, 92, 103, 105, 106, 108, 111–12, 114, 118, 119, 121–23

Pascall, Glenn, 30, 31, 49–50, 54, 62, 64, 68, 70,

Peirce, Neil R., 28, 36, 44, 95, 114

Pickens, T. Boone, 66–67, 140n

Pierce County, Wash., 36, 46, 93, 111

Plant relocation and recruitment, 109–10

Pluralist theory, xvii, xx–xxvi passim, 102–3, 126n

Political ecology, xxvi–xxvii, 104–5

Political economy. See Sell's Laws of Political Economy

Port of Seattle, 5, 80, 100

Ralston, Al, 71–73
Reich, Robert, 110
Renton, x, xxv, 5, 7–8, 18, 19, 20, 24, 50, 76, 78–85, 93, 112
Rodgers, Eugene, 26, 67
Ruckleshaus, William, 40
Rust, Nancy, 63

San Francisco, xix, xxv, 86, 110
Seattle, xii, xviii, x, xxi, xxiii, xxv, 5–7, 12–15, 16, 18–20, 22, 27, 29, 31, 34–37, 43–44, 57, 74–76, 77, 104, 119, 141n
Sell's Laws of Political Economy, xxvii–xxx, 11, 31, 60, 73, 104, 128n, 144n
747 jetliner, 26–27, 30, 42, 86–87, 88, 90
777 jetliner, 3, 30, 46, 49, 57, 83–84, 87–90, 92
Shrontz, Frank, 3–5, 16, 25, 26, 29, 46, 49, 50, 52, 53, 54, 61, 66–67, 69, 74, 76, 89, 91, 93–94, 96, 105–6, 112
Smith, Adam, 114–15
Society for Professional Engineering Employees in Aerospace, 58
South Carolina, 38,
State Environmental Policy Act (SEPA), 39, 95, 100–101
Stone, Clarence, xxviii

Taxes: and tax policy, 62–63, 66, 68, 79–80, 82, 112, 139n
Third face of power, 126n

Uhlman, Wes, 45, 69–70, 75
U.S. Air Mail Act, 18
U.S. Army Air Corps, 20

Volcker, Paul, 40

Wang, Art, 63
Washington Business Roundtable, 61, 99, 118–19
Washington State Research Council, 39–40
Webb, Sanford ("Sandy"), 81–82, 83, 103
Westervelt, G. Conrad, 13
Weyerhaeuser, 40, 68
Wichita, Kan., 21, 22, 49, 51, 89, 90, 105, 108
Wilson, T., 26, 47, 52, 55, 68
World War II, 18–19
Woodard, Ron, 26, 52, 112–13, 116–17